Advanced Programming
In MicroPython
by Example

By Yury Magda

To my wife, Julia

About the Author

Yury Magda is an embedded engineer experienced in designing hardware and software for Intel x86- and ARM-based mixed-signal systems. He is also the author of the books on designing embedded systems based upon Arduino, Raspberry Pi and BeagleBone Black development platforms.

Contents

Introduction...5
Disclaimer 5
Hardware and software 6
Upgrading Firmware 10
Designing high-performance MicroPython applications 17
Low-level programming General-Purpose I/O... 18
    Low-level programming digital outputs... 19
    Parallel processing several output pins... 30
    Low-level programming digital inputs 47
    Parallel processing several input pins.. 49
Programming external interrupts 54
    Optimizing ISR code 58
    External interrupts in measurement applications 60
Timing in MicroPython Applications.. 68
    Timers in loops and delays.. 68
    Measuring the pulse width of signals... 78
    Measuring the period of pulse trains 90
    Programming PWM... 95
Direct Digital Synthesis in MicroPython Applicatons.................................. 105
Analog-To-Digital Conversion in MicroPython applications 117
Conclusion 135
Index 136

Introduction

Nowadays MicroPython is becoming one of the most popular programming tools for embedded systems. MicroPython allows you to control hardware connected to the MicroPython board, write code modules expanding the features of your program, store them on an SD card for later use, and much more. MicroPython comes with modules for interacting with the hardware such as interrupts, timers, LEDs, ADC, DAC, PWM and other peripherals. Virtually MicroPython allows you to gain complete and direct control of the hardware, but in practice many essential capabilities of MicroPython remain unused. This book aims to cover many hidden aspects of hardware control and code optimization for the popular boards based upon the STM32F4xx microcontrollers.

This book is not for absolute beginners. It is assumed that you already have some experience and practical skills in MicroPython programming and understand the basics of Cortex-M MCU. The material of this book will also be useful for those who want to understand how the Cortex-M peripherals such as I/O ports, Timers, Analog-To-Digital and Digital-To-Analog converters work.

The book contains numerous code examples and tips that may help the readers in designing measurement and control applications in MicroPython. The book is written by the professional embedded engineer experienced over 20 years in designing embedded systems.

Disclaimer

While the author has used good faith efforts to ensure that the information and instructions contained in this book are accurate, the author disclaims all responsibility for errors or omissions, including without limitation responsibility for damages resulting from the use of or reliance on this work. Use of the information and instructions contained in this work is at your own risk. If any code samples or other technology this book contains or describes is subject to open source licenses or the intellectual property rights of others, it is your responsibility to ensure that your use thereof complies with such licenses and/or rights. All example applications from this book were developed and tested using the Pyboard v1.1 (PYBv1.1) and STM32F407DISCOVERY Development boards without damaging

5

hardware. The author will not accept any responsibility for damages of any kind due to actions taken by you after reading this book.

Hardware and software

The material of this book is based upon using a popular Pyboard v1.1 (PyBv1.1) development board and STM32F4DISCOVERY Discovery kit. Both tools are described in detail on www.micropython.org and www.st.com, respectively.

The PYBv1.1 board shown in **Fig.1** is a compact and powerful electronics development board that runs MicroPython. It connects to your PC over USB, giving you a USB flash drive to save your MicroPython scripts, and a serial Python prompt (a REPL) for instant programming.

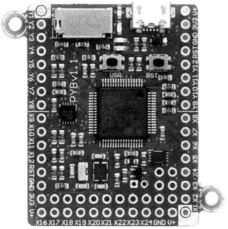

Fig.1

MicroPython runs bare-metal on the PYBv1.1, and essentially gives you a Python operating system. The built-in **pyb** module contains functions and classes to control the peripherals available on the board, such as UART, I2C, SPI, ADC and DAC.

There are 3 main ways to control the PYBv1.1 board:

- **REPL**: Connecting to your PC via USB, the board appears as a USB virtual COM port (CDC VCP) and you can use any serial program to connect and get a Python REPL prompt. This allows you to instantly type and execute Python commands, just like you would when running Python on your PC. You can also redirect the REPL to any of the UARTs on the Pyboard.

- **Remote script**: You can change from REPL to raw REPL mode by sending Ctrl-A, and then in raw REPL mode you can send an arbitrary Python script to the board for it to execute immediately. A Python script is available which makes using this mode very simple: you just run python pyboard.py script_to_run.py and this will execute script_to_run.py on the PYBv1.1, returning any output.

- **From file**: PYBv1.1 has a small, built-in file system which lives in part of the flash memory of the microcontroller. It also has an SD card slot if you want to extend the available storage. When you connect the PYBv1.1 to your PC, it appears as a USB flash storage device and you can access (mount) the internal file system and the SD card this way. If you copy a Python script to the file system and call it main.py, then the board will execute this script when it starts up. This way you can run scripts without being connected to a PC.

The heart of the PYBv1.1 board is the STM32F405RG microcontroller. That is a 168 MHz Cortex M4 MCU with hardware floating point, 1024KiB flash ROM and 192KiB RAM.

The board is equipped with a Micro USB connector for power and serial communication and Micro SD card slot, supporting standard and high capacity SD cards. The following peripherals are also available:

- 3-axis accelerometer (MMA7660);
- Real time clock with optional battery backup;
- 24 GPIO on left and right edges and 5 GPIO on bottom row, plus LED and switch GPIO available on bottom row;
- 3x 12-bit analog to digital converters, available on 16 pins, 4 with analog ground shielding;
- 2x 12-bit digital to analog (DAC) converters, available on pins X5 and X6;
- 4 LEDs (red, green, yellow and blue);
- 1 reset and 1 user switch.

The board is powered by the on-board 3.3V LDO voltage regulator, capable of supplying up to 250mA, input voltage range 3.6V to 16V. To upgrade firmware, we can use the DFU bootloader in ROM.

The following diagram (**Fig.2**) shows the pin configuration of the PYBv1.1.

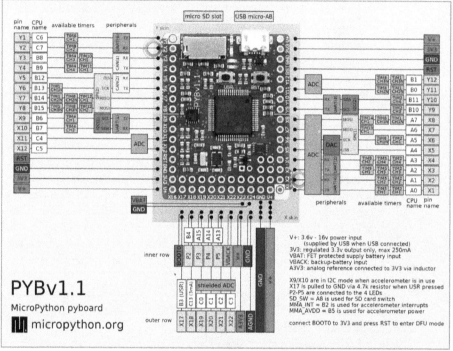

Fig.2

Our examples will frequently use the LEDs and user input switch, therefore **Table 1** details the pin assignment for these peripherals.

Table 1. Pin assignments for PYBv1.1

Peripherals	MCU pin
Input USR switch	B3
Blue LED	B4
Orange LED	A15
Red LED	A14
Green LED	A13

In this book, we also use one more board to run MicroPython applications – STM32F4DISCOVERY Discovery kit (**Fig.3**) equipped with the STM32F407VG high performance microcontroller with the ARM® Cortex®-M4 32-bit core.

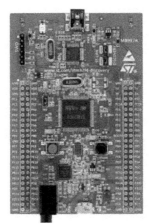

Fig.3

The STM32F4DISCOVERY offers the following features:

- STM32F407VGT6 microcontroller featuring 32-bit ARM Cortex-M4 with FPU core, 1-Mbyte Flash memory, 192-Kbyte RAM in an LQFP100 package;
- On-board ST-LINK/V2 on STM32F4DISCOVERY or ST-LINK/V2-A on STM32F407G-DISC1;
- USB ST-LINK with re-enumeration capability and three different interfaces:
  - Virtual COM port (with ST-LINK/V2-A only);
  - Mass storage (with ST-LINK/V2-A only);
  - Debug port;
- Board power supply:
  - Through USB bus;
  - External power sources:
    3 V and 5 V.
- LIS302DL or LIS3DSH ST MEMS 3-axis accelerometer;
- MP45DT02 ST MEMS audio sensor omni-directional digital microphone;
- CS43L22 audio DAC with integrated class D speaker driver;
- Eight LEDs:
  - LD1 (red/green) for USB communication;
  - LD2 (red) for 3.3 V power on;
  - Four user LEDs, LD3 (orange), LD4 (green), LD5 (red) and LD6 (blue);

– 2 USB OTG LEDs LD7 (green) VBUS and LD8 (red) over-current;
- Two push buttons (user and reset);
- USB OTG FS with micro-AB connector.

Before starting development MicroPython applications on development boards, we need to prepare firmware. The following section describes in brief how to upgrade the firmware for PYBv1.1 board and STM32F4DISCOVERY Discovery kit.

Upgrading Firmware

The easiest way to upgrade firmware for PYBv1.1 and STM32F4DISCOVERY is to use the STM32 DFU firmware upgrade tool (utility DfuSe) available on http://www.st.com/en/development-tools/stsw-stm32080.html. At the moment when this book was writing, the latest available version of the DfuSe utility was v3.0.6.

Let's consider upgrading firmware for PYBv1.1. First, we should download the latest version of firmware for PYBv1.1 from http://micropython.org/download.
Next, prepare PYBv1.1 by connecting the **BOOT** pin to **3.3V** pin (**Fig.4**), then connect the board to the PC by micro-USB cable.

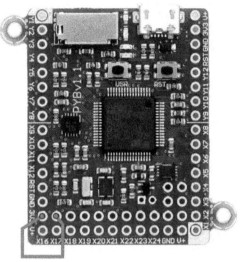

Fig.4

If PYBv1.1 is already connected to the PC, simply press/release the RST
button. Once you have done this, PYBv1.1 starts running a special DFU
program from ROM (read only memory) inside the STM32 MCU. This way
we can always replace MicroPython if it is broken for some reason.
In Windows, we can check that STM32 device is put in DFU mode through
'Device Manager'. In Windows 10, this device appears under
'Universal Serial Bus Controllers' (Fig.5).

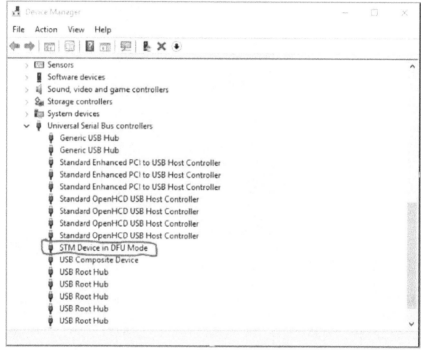

Fig.5

Then launch the DfuSe utility. Note that if some device in DFU mode is present, DfuSe reports that (**Fig.6**).

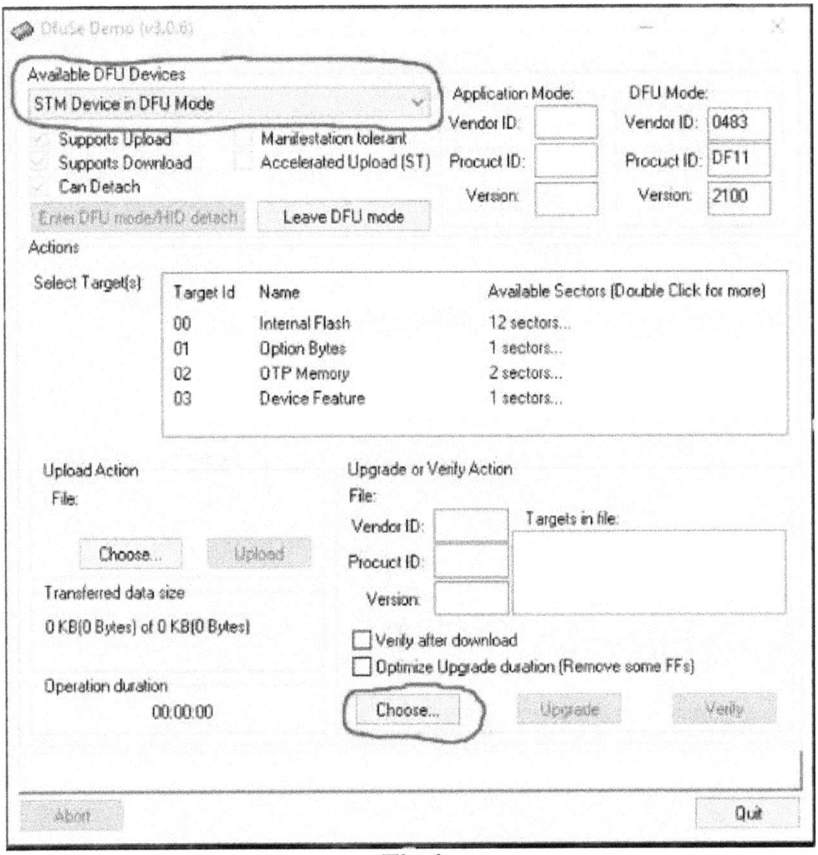

Fig.6

If some error occurs, the field '**Available DFU devices**' will be empty. If OK, we should select the desired .dfu file by pressing '**Choose...**' button, then press '**Upgrade**'. With default options, the upgrade process is running as is shown in **Fig.7**-**Fig.9**.

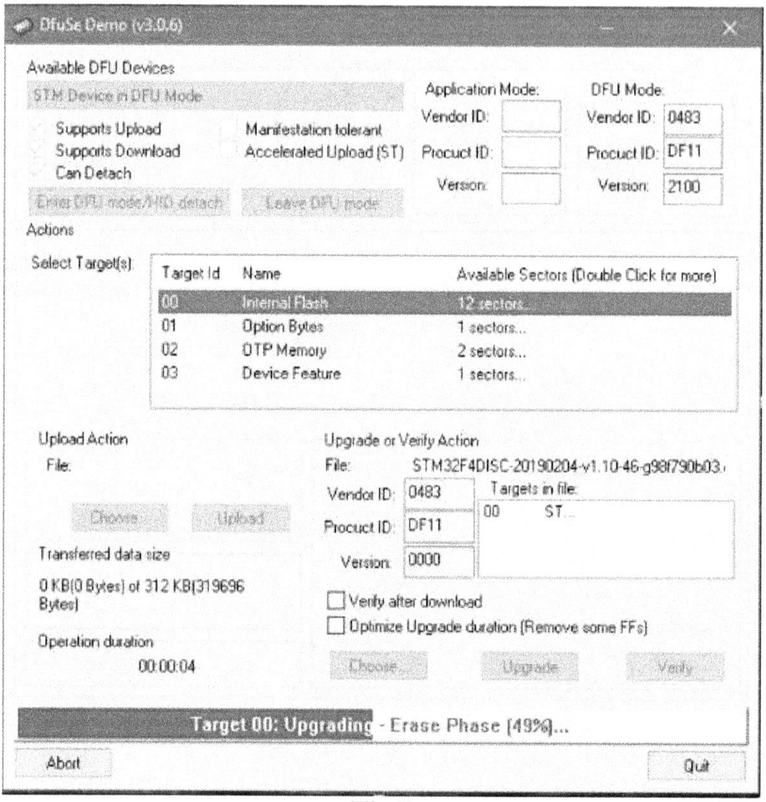

Fig.7

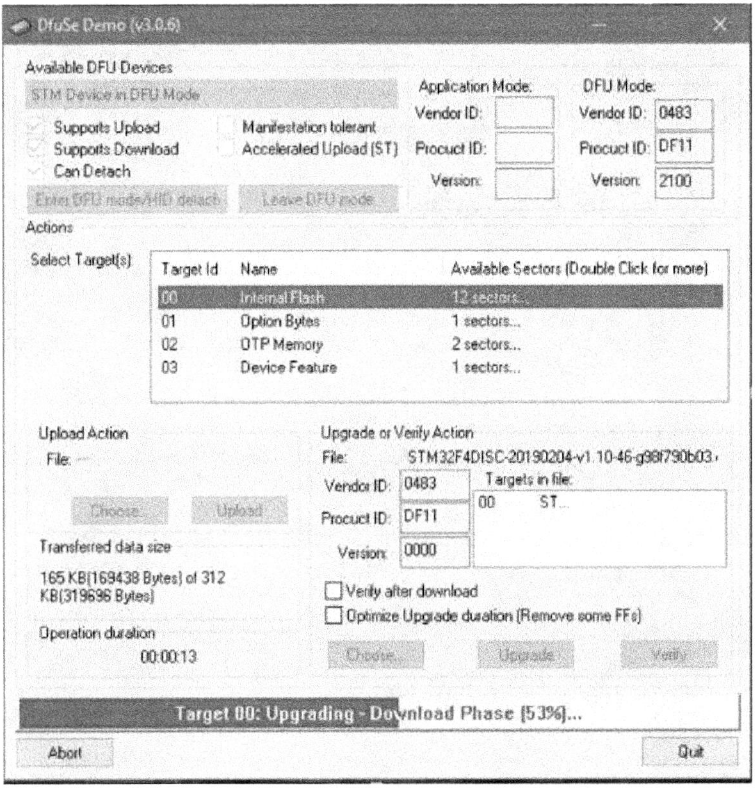

Fig.8

Fig.9

After upgrade is complete, check the '**Transferred data size**' – this should be the same size as that of the .**dfu** file.

Let's consider firmware upgrade of the STM32F4DISCOVERY Discovery Kit. First, download the latest version of firmware for STM32F4DISCOVERY from http://micropython.org/download, then prepare the board as follows:

- connect pins **BOOT0** and **VDD**;
- connect pins **3V** and **PA9**.

These connections are shown in **Fig.10**. Next, plug micro-USB cable into **CN5** and the other side of the USB cable into the computer.

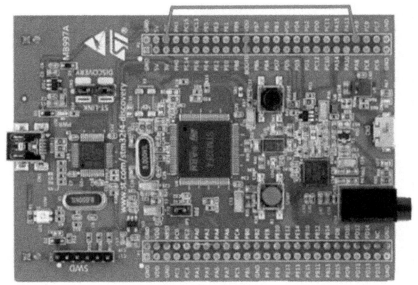

Fig.10

The following steps are the same as those for the PYBv1.1 board.

Designing high-performance MicroPython applications

There are various ways to achieve high performance of MicroPython applications. In this book, we consider the optimization methods based upon use of low-level programming techniques. MicroPython provides two powerful tools for writing fast code using low-level functions:

- the **machine** module that contains specific functions related to the hardware on a particular board. Most functions in this module allow to achieve direct and unrestricted access to and control of hardware blocks on a system (like MCU, GPIO, timers, ADC, etc.);
- the **inline assembler** that allows to access hardware using the low-level MCU instructions.

Low-level programming comes into the category of more advanced programming and involves some knowledge of the target MCU. For the PYBv1.1 board, you need to know how to operate with STM32F405RGT6

(Cortex-M4) MCU hardware. When reading this guide, it would be wise to have both STM32F4xx Datasheet, Programming and Reference Manual before your eyes.

The programming techniques applied to MicroPython applications running on the PYBv1.1 board, will also be applied to any boards equipped with the similar MCU (STM32F405/407).
Particularly, all MicroPython applications described in this guide will also run on STM32F4DISCOVERY board (STM32F407VGT6 MCU). What you only need to do is check the pin definitions for STM32F4DISCOVERY – these may be a bit different as compared with PYBv1.1.

Low-level programming General-Purpose I/O

The memory-mapped registers are often used in place of registers in the core, especially in industrial microcontrollers that have many peripherals, each with its own set of unique registers. General-purpose I/O (GPIO) as any other on-chip peripheral device is controlled through the set of 32-bit registers. Each general-purpose I/O port has the following registers:
- GPIO port mode register (GPIOx_MODER) (x = A..I/J/K);
- GPIO port output type register (GPIOx_OTYPER) (x = A..I/J/K);
- GPIO port output speed register (GPIOx_OSPEEDR) (x = A..I/J/K);
- GPIO port pull-up/pull-down register (GPIOx_PUPDR) (x = A..I/J/K);
- GPIO port input data register (GPIOx_IDR) (x = A..I/J/K);
- GPIO port output data register (GPIOx_ODR) (x = A..I/J/K);
- GPIO port bit set/reset register (GPIOx_BSRR) (x = A..I/J/K);
- GPIO port configuration lock register (GPIOx_LCKR) (x = A..I/J/K);
- GPIO alternate function low register (GPIOx_AFRL) (x = A..I/J/K);
- GPIO alternate function high register (GPIOx_AFRH) (x = A..I/J).

Each register from this set provides specific functions for an GPIO pin. These functions are detailed in the **Table 2**.

Table 2. GPIO register functions

Register	Function
GPIOx_MODER	Allows to configure the I/O direction mode (input, general purpose output mode, alternate function mode or analog mode)
GPIOx_OTYPER	Allows to configure the output type of the I/O port (output push-pull or output open-drain)
GPIOx_OSPEEDR	Allows to configure the I/O output speed (low, medium, high or very high)
GPIOx_PUPDR	Allows to configure the I/O pull-up or pull-down (no pull-up/pull-down, pull-up, pull-down)
GPIOx_IDR	Input data are brought here
GPIOx_ODR	Output data are written here
GPIOx_BSRR	Allows to perform bitwise write access to the particular bit in register GPIOx_ODR
GPIOx_LCKR	Used to lock the configuration of the port bits
GPIOx_AFRL	Allows to configure alternate I/O function for the low 8 bits
GPIOx_AFRH	Allows to configure alternate I/O function for the high 8 bits

Each I/O port bit is freely programmable, however the I/O port registers have to be accessed as 32-bit words, half-words or bytes. The purpose of the GPIOx_BSRR register is to allow atomic read/modify accesses to any of the GPIO registers. In this way, there is no risk of an interrupt occurring between the read and the modify access.

In MicroPython, class Pin is used to control GPIO pins. It has methods (functions) to set the mode of the pin (input, output, etc.) and methods to get and set the digital logic level.

Using direct access to GPIO registers with low-level or inline assembler instructions gives a developer flexible control over GPIO ports and pins and allows to write fast code for I/O operations.

In the following sections, we will consider how to perform low-level I/O operations on digital pins.

Low-level programming digital outputs

This section describes how to write fast code for control of digital outputs of the MCU. The programming techniques based on understanding the architecture of microcontroller STM32F405/407 (Cortex-M4).
In MicroPython, configuring the I/O pin for output using high-level statements is very simple. For example, to configure pin PB4 of the PYBv1.1 board as output, we need to execute the sequence:

```
from pyb import Pin
p_out = Pin('B4', Pin.OUT_PP)
```

The same task can be implemented by applying low-level functions from the **machine** module (**Listing 1**). In this case, we gain direct access to the GPIO registers, thus increasing the performance of code.

Listing 1.

```
machine.mem32[stm.RCC + stm.RCC_AHB1ENR] |= 1<<1
machine.mem32[stm.GPIOB + stm.GPIO_MODER] |= 1<<8
machine.mem32[stm.GPIOB + stm.GPIO_OTYPER] &= ~(1<<4)
machine.mem32[stm.GPIOB + stm.GPIO_OSPEEDR] |= 2<<8
machine.mem32[stm.GPIOB + stm.GPIO_PUPDR] &= ~(3<<8)
```

In this code, we use the **stm** module which provides a set of constants for easy access to the registers of the STM32F4xx MCU. The **mem32** method allows to get the 32-bit data held at some 32-bit memory address. The **machine** module also provides the **mem16** and **mem8** methods for access 16- and 8-bit data at 32-bit memory address, respectively.

The set of registers associated with any peripheral device (GPIO, timer, etc.) is mapped into memory. Each set of registers has its own base address in memory, so any register in the set can be reached through some predetermined offset. In our example, we should access the RCC and GPIOB registers with their boundary addresses taken from the datasheet on STM32F405/407 MCU (**Fig.11**).

0x4002 3800 - 0x4002 3BFF	RCC	
0x4002 3000 - 0x4002 33FF	CRC	AHB1
0x4002 2800 - 0x4002 2BFF	GPIOK	
0x4002 2400 - 0x4002 27FF	GPIOJ	
0x4002 2000 - 0x4002 23FF	GPIOI	
0x4002 1C00 - 0x4002 1FFF	GPIOH	
0x4002 1800 - 0x4002 1BFF	GPIOG	
0x4002 1400 - 0x4002 17FF	GPIOF	
0x4002 1000 - 0x4002 13FF	GPIOE	
0x4002 0C00 - 0x4002 0FFF	GPIOD	
0x4002 0800 - 0x4002 0BFF	GPIOC	
0x4002 0400 - 0x4002 07FF	GPIOB	
0x4002 0000 - 0x4002 03FF	GPIOA	

Fig.11

Let's back to our code. The first statement

machine.mem32[stm.RCC + stm.RCC_AHB1ENR] |= 1<<1

enables clocking to the port GPIOB. **Note** that all on-chip peripherals can operate only if they are clocked. Therefore, this statement enables clocking port GPIOB by setting bit 1 in the RCC AHB1 peripheral clock enable register (RCC_AHB1ENR). This register is accessed through the base address stm.RCC and offset stm.RCC_AHB1ENR.

It is easy to view the address of a particular register using the **print()** function. For example, the base address of the RCC register set will be determined as:

```
>>> print(hex(stm.RCC))
0x40023800
```

The offset of register RCC_AHB1ENR is determined as:

```
>>> print(hex(stm.RCC_AHB1ENR))
0x30
```

Therefore, the full address of the RCC_AHB1ENR register will be calculated as

stm.RCC + stm.RCC_AHB1ENR = 0x40023800 + 0x30

Some words about clocking on-chip peripherals. Usually, a clock source is connected to peripherals immediately after powering on or reset. Nevertheless, it you aren't confident about clocking, it would be better to enable clocking peripherals explicitly.

Once clocking the GPIOB port is enabled, we can configure pin PB4 for digital output.
The statement

machine.mem32[stm.GPIOB + stm.GPIO_MODER] |= 1<<8

from **Listing 1** defines the mode of bit 4 in the GPIO port mode register GPIO_MODER. In our case, we configure bit 4 of port GPIOB as a general purpose output by writing code 0b01 in the corresponding positions in GPIO_MODER.
The statement

machine.mem32[stm.GPIOB + stm.GPIO_OTYPER] &= ~(1<<4)

defines the type of output (push-pull, code 0) by writing the value ~(1<<4) into the corresponding position in the GPIO port output type register GPIO_OTYPER.
We also need to define the speed of the output pin. In this example, we set high speed by writing the value 0b10 into the corresponding position in the GPIO port output speed register GPIO_OSPEEDR. That is performed by the statement

machine.mem32[stm.GPIOB + stm.GPIO_OSPEEDR] |= 2<<8

The last statement in this sequence

machine.mem32[stm.GPIOB + stm.GPIO_PUPDR] &= ~(3<<8)

defines pull-up/pull-down option for the output pin. In our case, we select no pull-up/pull-down option by writing the value ~(3<<8) into the corresponding position in the GPIO port pull-up/pull-down register GPIO_PUPDR.

Once we have finished to configure pin PB4, we can test it. Recall that pin PB4 in PYBv1.1 drives the Blue LED. Now we are capable to drive the LED through register GPIO_ODR.
To drive the LED ON, we should set (=1) pin PB4 by the statement

machine.mem32[stm.GPIOB + stm.GPIO_ODR] |= 1<<4

To drive the LED OFF, we should clear (=0) pin PB4 by the statement

machine.mem32[stm.GPIOB + stm.GPIO_ODR] &= ~(1<<4)

If we need to toggle the LED, type in the following statement

machine.mem32[stm.GPIOB + stm.GPIO_ODR] ^= 1<<4

Alternatively, to drive pin PB4 ON/OFF, we can use the GPIO port bit set/reset register GPIOB_BSRR. In MicroPython, this register is represented as the pair of 16-bit registers, GPIO_BSRRH and GPIO_BSRRL.
We can set pin PB4 by writing 1 into 16-bit register GPIO_BSSL by the statement

machine.mem16[stm.GPIOB + stm.GPIO_BSRRL] |= 1<<4

Since we deal with 16-bit memory location, we use **mem16** method instead of **mem32**.
To clear pin PB4, we should write 1 into the proper position in register GPIO_BSRRH:

machine.mem16[stm.GPIOB + stm.GPIO_BSRRH] |= 1<<4

The fast code that uses physical addresses for direct access of pin PB4 is shown below (**Listing 2**).

Listing 2.

```
machine.mem32[0x40023800 + 0x30] |= 1<<1
machine.mem32[0x40020400 + 0x0] |= 1<<8
machine.mem32[0x40020400 + 0x4] &= ~(1<<4)
machine.mem32[0x40020400 + 0x8] |= 2<<8
machine.mem32[0x40020400 + 0xc] &= ~(3<<8)
```

Fast toggling pin PB4 through GPIO_ODR register can be performed by the statement:

```
machine.mem32[0x40020400 + 0x14] ^= 1<<4
```

The following example code (**Listing 3**) is written for the STM32F407DISCOVERY board. The sequence below configures pin PD13 (Orange LED) as digital output.

Listing 3.

```
machine.mem32[stm.RCC + stm.RCC_AHB1ENR] |= 1<<3
machine.mem32[stm.GPIOD + stm.GPIO_MODER] |= 1<<26
machine.mem32[stm.GPIOD + stm.GPIO_OTYPER] &= ~(1<<13)
machine.mem32[stm.GPIOD + stm.GPIO_OSPEEDR] |= 2<<26
machine.mem32[stm.GPIOD + stm.GPIO_PUPDR] &= ~(3<<26)
```

To test this configuration, let's try to toggle the LED attached to pin PD13 by the statement

```
machine.mem16[stm.GPIOD + stm.GPIO_ODR] ^= 1<<13
```

Another way to toggle the LED is to use the GPIO_BSRRL and GPIO_BSRRH registers:

```
machine.mem16[stm.GPIOD + stm.GPIO_BSRRL] |= 1<<13
machine.mem16[stm.GPIOD + stm.GPIO_BSRRH] |= 1<<13
```

The code developed using the low-level functions from the **machine** module runs fast enough, but we can achieve even better performance with the MiroPython inline assembler.

A MicroPython inline assembler allows you to write assembly routines as Python functions that can be invoked in a usual way. The inline assembler is a very powerful tool that increases the performance of an application and/or reduce the size of code.

Let's see how we can use the MicroPython inline assembler to control a digital output pin by rewriting the configuration procedure for pin PB4 of PYBv1.1 shown in **Listing 1**.

The inline assembler version of code is shown in **Listing 4**.

Listing 4.

```
@micropython.asm_thumb
def config_output_pin():
    movwt(r0, stm.RCC)
    ldr(r1, [r0, stm.RCC_AHB1ENR])
    movw(r2, 1<<1)
    orr(r1, r2)
    str(r1, [r0, stm.RCC_AHB1ENR])
    movwt(r0, stm.GPIOB)
    ldr(r1, [r0, stm.GPIO_MODER])
    movw(r2, 1<<8)
    orr(r1, r2)
    str(r1, [r0, stm.GPIO_MODER])
    ldr(r1, [r0, stm.GPIO_OTYPER])
    movw(r2, 1<<4)
    bic(r1, r2)
    str(r1, [r0, stm.GPIO_OTYPER])
    ldr(r1, [r0, stm.GPIO_OSPEEDR])
    movw(r2, 2<<8)
    orr(r1, r2)
    str(r1, [r0, stm.GPIO_OSPEEDR])
    ldr(r1, [r0, stm.GPIO_PUPDR])
    movw(r2, 3<<8)
    bic(r1, r2)
    str(r1, [r0, stm.GPIO_PUPDR])
```

To launch this function, use the syntax:

```
config_output_pin()
```

The **config_output_pin()** does the same job as the sequence shown in **Listing 1**, but will run a bit faster due to the following reason. The low-level functions such as

machine.mem8[]
machine.mem16[]
machine.mem32[]

are fast, but on the same GPIO port they perform additional operations while loading a base address of GPIO. Each time the **machine.mem[]** method is invoked, it loads the same base address of a GPIO port. For example, in the sequence from **Listing 1**, there will be 4 loading operations of the same GPIOB base address.

These operations waste the MCU time and decrease the overall performance of code. Using the inline assembler allows to avoid this problem as is illustrated by the code of the **config_output_pin()** function. In this function, the base address of port GPIOB is loaded only once, by the statement

movwt(r0, stm.GPIOB)

Then all further operations with the GPIOB registers (**ldr** and **str** instructions) use the same base address already loaded in the MCU register **r0**. This way the assembler code saves 3 extra instructions as compared with code from **Listing 1**.

Note that using the MicroPython inline assembler requires good understanding the STM32F4xx MCU architecture and instruction set. To write fast code in the inline assembler, you should carefully think of the algorithm of your application. Remember that the inline assembler is not panacea for developing fast code in all possible situations, though it can help in many cases.

Let's discuss how to implement fast write operations on the output pin using a MicroPython inline assembler.

The following functions (**Listing 5 – Listing 7**) written in the inline assembler allow to perform fast set, clear and toggle operations on pin PB4 of PYBv1.1.

To fast set (=1) pin PB4 (**Listing 5**), we can use function **set_output()** without parameters. This function operates with register GPIO_ODR of port GPIOB.

Listing 5.

```
@micropython.asm_thumb
def set_output():
    movwt(r0, stm.GPIOB)
    movw(r1, 1<<4)
    ldr(r2, [r0, stm.GPIO_ODR])
    orr(r2, r1)
    str(r2, [r0, stm.GPIO_ODR])
```

In this code, we use the assembler instruction

```
orr(r2, r1)
```

to set bit 4 of port GPIOB.
To run the above code, use the following syntax:

```
set_output()
```

To fast clear (=0) pin PB4 (**Listing 6**), we can use the code from **Listing 5** as a template where we should replace the assembler instruction

```
orr(r2, r1)
```

with

```
bic(r2, r1)
```

that clears bit 4 of port GPIOB.

Listing 6.

```
@micropython.asm_thumb
def clear_output():
    movwt(r0, stm.GPIOB)
    movw(r1, 1<<4)
```

```
ldr(r2, [r0, stm.GPIO_ODR])
bic(r2, r1)
str(r2, [r0, stm.GPIO_ODR])
```

To run the above code, use the following syntax:

```
clear_output()
```

To fast toggle pin PB4, we can use function **toggle_output()** whose inline assembler code is shown in **Listing 7**.

Listing 7.

```
@micropython.asm_thumb
def toggle_output():
    movwt(r0, stm.GPIOB)
    movw(r1, 1<<4)
    ldr(r2, [r0, stm.GPIO_ODR])
    eor(r2, r1)
    str(r2, [r0, stm.GPIO_ODR])
```

In this code, the assembler instruction

```
eor(r2, r1)
```

performs the bitwise exclusive OR operation on bit PB4 thus inverting it. To run the above code, use the syntax:

```
toggle_output()
```

Even more compact code for fast setting / clearing the digital output PB4 can be written if we use registers GPIO_BSRR[H/L] as is illustrated in **Listing 8 - 9**). The code below (function **set_output_1()**) allows to fast set pin PB4.

Listing 8.

```
@micropython.asm_thumb
def set_output_1():
    movwt(r0, stm.GPIOB)
```

```
movw(r1, 1<<4)
strh(r1, [r0, stm.GPIO_BSRRL])
```

Fast clearing pin PB4 is implemented by the **clear_output_1()** function from **Listing 9**.

Listing 9.

```
@micropython.asm_thumb
def clear_output_1():
    movwt(r0, stm.GPIOC)
    movw(r1, 1<<7)
    strh(r1, [r0, stm.GPIO_BSRRH])
```

Sometimes there may be no need to implement deep optimization of MicroPython code. In these cases, we can optimize particular fragments of code using the inline assembler or low-level functions from the **machine** module, while writing the less critical parts using high-level MicroPython programming constructions.

The following code (**Listing 10**) illustrates this concept. With this code, we can periodically set/clear pin PA15 (the Orange LED on the PYBv1.1 board). The initialization fragment of code is implemented using high-level MicroPython constructions, while the **write_pin()** function that should repeatedly set/clear PA14 is written in the inline assembler.
Function **write_pin()** takes a single parameter that may be assigned either 0 or 1. If the parameter = 0, **write_pin()** clears (=0) pin PA14 thus driving the LED OFF. If the parameter = 1, the function sets (=1) pin PA14 thus driving the LED ON.

Listing 10.

```
from pyb import LED
import time
orangeLED = LED(3)
@micropython.asm_thumb
def write_pin(r0):
    movwt(r1, stm.GPIOA)
    ldr(r2, [r1, stm.GPIO_ODR])
    movw(r3, 1<<15)
```

```
    cmp(r0, 1)
    ite(eq)
    orr(r2, r3)
    bic(r2, r3)
    strh(r2, [r1, stm.GPIO_ODR])
while True:
    write_pin(1)
    time.sleep_ms(500)
    write_pin(0)
    time.sleep_ms(1500)
```

Parallel processing several output pins

Often we need to control several digital outputs at a time. MicroPython, however, doesn't have a class capable of implementing this task. Nevertheless, we can easily write data into several bits of GPIO port at a time using the MicroPython low-level functions or inline assembler instructions.

The below examples (**Listing 11**-**13**) show the programming techniques for accessing several bits at a time on port GPIOA. To perform this task, the GPIO port bit set/reset register (GPIOx_BSRR) is used.
The fragment of code shown in **Listing 11** allows to set 3 bits of port GPIOA. Function **set_bits()** when invoked sets bits PA13 (Green LED), PA14 (Red LED) and PA15 (Orange LED) at a time.

Listing 11.

```
from pyb import Pin
pGreen = Pin('A13', Pin.OUT_PP)
pRed = Pin('A14', Pin.OUT_PP)
pOrange = Pin('A15', Pin.OUT_PP)
@micropython.asm_thumb
def set_bits():
    movwt(r0, stm.GPIOA)
    movw(r1, 7<<13)
    strh(r1, [r0, stm.GPIO_BSRRL])
```

In this code, the value 7 is shifted to the corresponding positions in the low word GPIO_BSRRL of register GPIO_BSRR to set bits PA13-PA15. Function **clear_bits()** from **Listing 12** allows to clear these 3 bits of port GPIOA at a time.

Listing 12.

```
from pyb import Pin
pGreen = Pin('A13', Pin.OUT_PP)
pRed = Pin('A14', Pin.OUT_PP)
pOrange = Pin('A15', Pin.OUT_PP)
@micropython.asm_thumb
def clear_bits():
    movwt(r0, stm.GPIOA)
    movw(r1, 7<<13)
    strh(r1, [r0, stm.GPIO_BSRRH])
```

In this code, we shift the value 7 to the corresponding positions in the high word GPIO_BSRRH of register GPIO_BSRR that affects bits A31-A29.

The function **toggle_bits()** whose code is shown in **Listing 13** allows to fast toggle several digital outputs at a time. As in the previous example, we will use the PYBv1.1 on-board LEDs to illustrate the approach. With this code, we will toggle bits PA13 (Green LED), PA14 (Red LED) and PA15 (Orange LED) at a time.

Listing 13.

```
from pyb import Pin
pGreen = Pin('A13', Pin.OUT_PP)
pRed = Pin('A14', Pin.OUT_PP)
pOrange = Pin('A15', Pin.OUT_PP)
@micropython.asm_thumb
def toggle_bits(r0):
    cmp(r0, 1)
    bgt(exit)
    cmp(r0, 0)
    blt(exit)
    movwt(r1, stm.GPIOA)
    movw(r2, 7<<13)
```

```
        cmp(r0, 0)
        ite(eq)
        strh(r2, [r1, stm.GPIO_BSRRH])
        strh(r2, [r1, stm.GPIO_BSRRL])
        label(exit)
```

In this code, function **toggle_bits()** takes a single parameter that can be assigned either 0 or 1. If the parameter = 0, the function clears pins PA13-PA15. If the parameter = 1, the function sets these pins.
To set pins PA13-PA15 (drive LEDs ON), use the following syntax:

toggle_bits(1)

To clear pins PA13-PA15 (drive LEDs OFF), enter

toggle_bits(0)

Below (**Listing 14**) is the modified version of the **toggle_bits()** function adapted for the STM32F407DISCOVERY board where on-board LEDs are connected to pins PD12-PD15 of port GPIOD.

Listing 14.

```
from pyb import Pin
pGreen = Pin('PD12', Pin.OUT_PP)
pOrange = Pin('PD13', Pin.OUT_PP)
pRed = Pin('PD14', Pin.OUT_PP)
pBlue = Pin('PD15', Pin.OUT_PP)
@micropython.asm_thumb
def toggle_bits(r0):
    cmp(r0, 1)
    bgt(exit)
    cmp(r0, 0)
    blt(exit)
    movwt(r1, stm.GPIOD)
    movw(r2, 15<<12)
    cmp(r0, 0)
    ite(eq)
    strh(r2, [r1, stm.GPIO_BSRRH])
    strh(r2, [r1, stm.GPIO_BSRRL])
```

label(exit)

Alternatively, instead of register GPIO_BSRR we can use GPIO_ODR with corresponding changes in code as is shown in **Listing 15 – Listing 17**. This code is adapted to the STM32F407DISCOVERY board.
Function **set_bits_1()** whose code is shown in **Listing 15** allows to set several digital outputs at a time using register GPIO_ODR.

Listing 15.

```
from pyb import Pin
pGreen = Pin('PD12', Pin.OUT_PP)
pOrange = Pin('PD13', Pin.OUT_PP)
pRed = Pin('PD14', Pin.OUT_PP)
pBlue = Pin('PD15', Pin.OUT_PP)
@micropython.asm_thumb
def set_bits_1():
    movwt(r0, stm.GPIOD)
    ldr(r1, [r0, stm.GPIO_ODR])
    movw(r2, 15<<12)
    orr(r1, r2)
    str(r1, [r0, stm.GPIO_ODR])
```

Function **clear_bits_1()** from **Listing 16** uses register GPIO_ODR to clear several digital outputs at a time.

Listing 16.

```
from pyb import Pin
pGreen = Pin('PD12', Pin.OUT_PP)
pOrange = Pin('PD13', Pin.OUT_PP)
pRed = Pin('PD14', Pin.OUT_PP)
pBlue = Pin('PD15', Pin.OUT_PP)
@micropython.asm_thumb
def clear_bits_1():
    movwt(r0, stm.GPIOD)
    ldr(r1, [r0, stm.GPIO_ODR])
    movw(r2, 15<<12)
    bic(r1, r2)
    str(r1, [r0, stm.GPIO_ODR])
```

The source code of function **write_bits_1 (Listing 17)** allows to either clear or set digital outputs PD12-PD15 of STM32F4DISCOVERY at a time.

Listing 17.

```
from pyb import Pin
pGreen = Pin('PD12', Pin.OUT_PP)
pOrange = Pin('PD13', Pin.OUT_PP)
pRed = Pin('PD14', Pin.OUT_PP)
pBlue = Pin('PD15', Pin.OUT_PP)
@micropython.asm_thumb
def write_bits_1(r0):
    cmp(r0, 1)
    bgt(exit)
    cmp(r0, 0)
    blt(exit)
    movwt(r1, stm.GPIOD)
    movw(r2, 15<<12)
    ldr(r3, [r1, stm.GPIO_ODR])
    cmp(r0, 0)
    ite(eq)
    bic(r3, r2)
    orr(r3, r2)
    strh(r3, [r1, stm.GPIO_ODR])
    label(exit)
```

In this code, function **write_bits_1()** takes either 0 or 1 as a parameter that is passed in the CPU register **r0**.
The following sequence at the beginning of code

```
cmp(r0, 1)
bgt(exit)
cmp(r0, 0)
blt(exit)
```

checks if the parameter equals 0 or 1. If both conditions are false, the code loads the value of register GPIO_ODR in the MCU register **r3** and saves the bitmask for bits (pins) PD12-PD15 in the MCU register **r2**. This is performed by the following sequence:

```
movwt(r1, stm.GPIOD)
movw(r2, 15<<12)
ldr(r3, [r1, stm.GPIO_ODR])
```

Then the code sets or clears the selected bits in MCU register **r3** depending on the value held in MCU register **r0**. This is done by the sequence:

```
cmp(r0, 0)
ite(eq)
bic(r3, r2)
orr(r3, r2)
```

Notice that the **ite()** assembler instruction in this fragment provides the conditional execution - this way we can eliminate extra branches in code thus increasing the performance of an application.
Finally, the new value is written back into register GPIO_ODR by the statement:

```
strh(r3, [r1, stm.GPIO_ODR])
```

The code in **Listing 18** shows how to set digital outputs on the GPIOD port of STM32F407DISCOVERY in the predetermined order.

Listing 18.

```
from pyb import Pin
pGreen = Pin('PD12', Pin.OUT_PP)
pOrange = Pin('PD13', Pin.OUT_PP)
pRed = Pin('PD14', Pin.OUT_PP)
pBlue = Pin('PD15', Pin.OUT_PP)
@micropython.asm_thumb
def write_bits_2(r0):
    movwt(r1, stm.GPIOD)
    ldr(r2, [r1, stm.GPIO_ODR])
    movw(r3, 0xf<<12)
    bic(r2, r3)
    lsl(r0, r0, 12)
    orr(r2, r0)
    strh(r2, [r1, stm.GPIO_ODR])
```

In this code, function **write_bits_2()** takes a single parameter that can be assigned the value in the range 0-15.
Initially, the contents of the GPIO data register GPIO_ODR is loaded in the MCU register **r2** by the instruction

```
ldr(r2, [r1, stm.GPIO_ODR])
```

Then the following sequence clears bits PD12-PD15 using the bitmask held in register **r3**:

```
movw(r3, 0xf<<12)
bic(r2, r3)
```

The sequence that follows sets the desired bits in positions [PD12:PD15] according to the parameter passed to function **write_bits_2()** in register **r0**:

```
lsl(r0, r0, 12)
orr(r2, r0)
strh(r2, [r1, stm.GPIO_ODR])
```

To set the proper parameter of the function **write_bits_2()**, we can select the suitable bitmask from **Table 3**.

Table 3. Bitmask combinations for pins PD12-PD15

Parameter	Pin PD12	Pin PD13	Pin PD14	Pin PD15
0	cleared	cleared	cleared	cleared
1	set	cleared	cleared	cleared
2	cleared	set	cleared	cleared
3	set	set	cleared	cleared
4	cleared	cleared	set	cleared
5	set	cleared	set	cleared
6	cleared	set	set	cleared
7	set	set	set	cleared
8	cleared	cleared	cleared	set
9	set	cleared	cleared	set
10	cleared	set	cleared	set
11	set	set	cleared	set
12	cleared	cleared	set	set
13	set	cleared	set	set

| 14 | cleared | set | set | set |
| 15 | set | set | set | set |

For example, the following statement

write_bits_2(0)

clears all pins (PD12-PD15).
The statement

write_bits_2(3)

sets pins PD12 (Green LED) and PD13 (Orange LED).
The statement

write_bits_2(11)

sets pins PD12 (Green LED), PD13(Orange LED) and PD15(Blue LED).
The statement

write_bits_2(15)

sets all pins (PD12-PD15).

In **Listing 19** there is the code of a **write_bits_2()** function that controls the PYBv1.1 on-board LEDs (pins PA13-PA15).

Listing 19.

```
from pyb import Pin
pGreen = Pin('A13', Pin.OUT_PP)
pRed = Pin('A14', Pin.OUT_PP)
pOrange = Pin('A15', Pin.OUT_PP)
@micropython.asm_thumb
def write_bits_2(r0):
    movwt(r1, stm.GPIOA)
    ldr(r2, [r1, stm.GPIO_ODR])
    movw(r3, 7<<13)
    bic(r2, r3)
    lsl(r0, r0, 13)
```

```
orr(r2, r0)
strh(r2, [r1, stm.GPIO_ODR])
```

In this code, we set /clear pins PA13 (Green LED), PA14(Red LED) and PA15(Orange LED), therefore the parameter passed to the **write_bits_2()** function can change in the range of 0-7.

To set the proper parameter of the function **write_bits_2()**, we can select the suitable bitmask from **Table 4**.

Table 4. Bitmask combinations for pins PA13-PA15

Parameter	Pin PA13	Pin PA14	Pin PA15
0	cleared	cleared	cleared
1	set	cleared	cleared
2	cleared	set	cleared
3	set	set	cleared
4	cleared	cleared	set
5	set	cleared	set
6	cleared	set	set
7	set	set	set

For example, the statement

write_bits_2(0)

clears all pins (PA13-PA15).
The statement

write_bits_2(3)

sets pins PA13 (Green LED) and PA14 (Red LED).
The statement

write_bits_2(6)

sets pins PA14 (Red LED) and PA15(Orange LED).
The statement

write_bits_2(7)

sets all pins (PA13-PA15).

In the previous examples, we used the **stm** module for access to the memory mapped registers of the STM32F4xx MCU. It is possible, however, to access registers explicitly using their physical addresses. That allows to make a MicroPython code a bit faster.
The examples below illustrate this concept.
In the first example we want to control pins of port GPIOD on the STM32F407DISCOVERY board. To determine the physical addresses of the registers relating to port GPIOD, we should find to the 'Memory map' section in the Reference Manual on STM32F405/407 MCU (**Fig.12**).

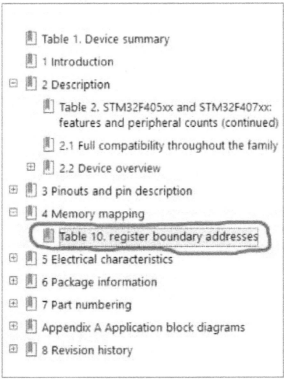

Fig.12

Note that there exist a few versions of Reference Manual with different enumerations of sections. In my case, I found the required information in

Table 10 of the Manual. In this table, the record relating to port GPIOD looks like the following (**Fig.13**).

	0x4002 6000 - 0x4002 63FF	DMA1
	0x4002 5000 - 0x4002 5FFF	Reserved
	0x4002 4000 - 0x4002 4FFF	BKPSRAM
AHB1	0x4002 3C00 - 0x4002 3FFF	Flash interface register
	0x4002 3800 - 0x4002 3BFF	RCC
	0x4002 3400 - 0x4002 37FF	Reserved
	0x4002 3000 - 0x4002 33FF	CRC
	0x4002 2400 - 0x4002 2FFF	Reserved
	0x4002 2000 - 0x4002 23FF	GPIOI
	0x4002 1C00 - 0x4002 1FFF	GPIOH
	0x4002 1800 - 0x4002 1BFF	GPIOG
	0x4002 1400 - 0x4002 17FF	GPIOF
	0x4002 1000 - 0x4002 13FF	GPIOE
	0x4002 0C00 - 0x4002 0FFF	GPIOD
	0x4002 0800 - 0x4002 0BFF	GPIOC
	0x4002 0400 - 0x4002 07FF	GPIOB

Fig.13

It may be helpful at this point to introduce the term 'effective address' that is often used to describe the final address created from values in the various registers, with offsets and/or shifts.

It is seen that the base address of port GPIOD is 0x40020C00. In our example we will use the data register GPIO_ODR, therefore we should calculate its effective address. This address will be simply a sum of the base address of GPIOD and the address offset of register GPIO_ODR. These values can be found in the Reference Manual on STM32F4xx Processors in the 'GPIO registers' section (**Fig.14**).

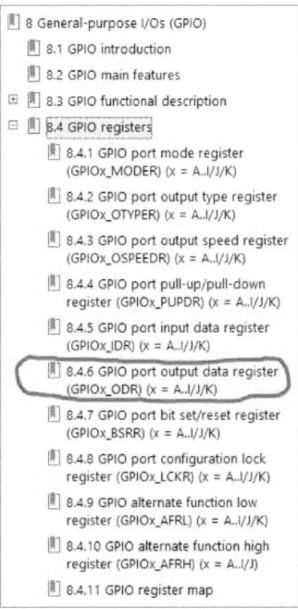

8 General-purpose I/Os (GPIO)

8.1 GPIO introduction

8.2 GPIO main features

8.3 GPIO functional description

8.4 GPIO registers

8.4.1 GPIO port mode register (GPIOx_MODER) (x = A..I/J/K)

8.4.2 GPIO port output type register (GPIOx_OTYPER) (x = A..I/J/K)

8.4.3 GPIO port output speed register (GPIOx_OSPEEDR) (x = A..I/J/K)

8.4.4 GPIO port pull-up/pull-down register (GPIOx_PUPDR) (x = A..I/J/K)

8.4.5 GPIO port input data register (GPIOx_IDR) (x = A..I/J/K)

8.4.6 GPIO port output data register (GPIOx_ODR) (x = A..I/J/K)

8.4.7 GPIO port bit set/reset register (GPIOx_BSRR) (x = A..I/J/K)

8.4.8 GPIO port configuration lock register (GPIOx_LCKR) (x = A..I/J/K)

8.4.9 GPIO alternate function low register (GPIOx_AFRL) (x = A..I/J/K)

8.4.10 GPIO alternate function high register (GPIOx_AFRH) (x = A..I/J)

8.4.11 GPIO register map

Fig.14

Finally, we get the address offset of register GPIO_ODR (**Fig.15**) that is 0x14.

41

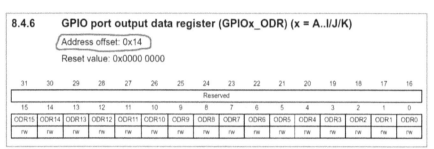

Fig.15

Now we have all required information and can write the MicroPython code for driving the pins of port GPIOD. Function **write_bits_3()** from **Listing 20** takes a single parameter that can be assigned the values in the range of 0-15.

For example, if the parameter = 0, the function clears bits PD12-PD14 thus driving all STM32F4DISCOVERY LEDs OFF. If the parameter = 5, the code sets bits PD12 and PD14. With the parameter equal to 15, bits PD12-PD15 are all set (all LEDs are ON), etc.

Listing 20.

```
from pyb import Pin
pGreen = Pin('PD12', Pin.OUT_PP)
pOrange = Pin('PD13', Pin.OUT_PP)
pRed = Pin('PD14', Pin.OUT_PP)
pBlue = Pin('PD15', Pin.OUT_PP)
@micropython.asm_thumb
def write_bits_3(r0):
    movwt(r1, 0x4002<<16)
    movw(r2, 0x0c00)
    add(r1, r1, r2)
    ldr(r2, [r1, 0x14])
    movw(r3, 0xf<<12)
    bic(r2, r3)
    lsl(r0, r0, 12)
    orr(r2, r0)
    strh(r2, [r1, 0x14])
```

At the beginning of this code, pins PD12-PD15 are configured as outputs by the MicroPython high-level statements. The following inline assembler instructions

```
movwt(r1, 0x4002<<16)
movw(r2, 0x0c00)
add(r1, r1, r2)
```

load the address of register GPIO_ODR in the MCU register **r1**.
Then the contents of GPIO_ODR is loaded in MCU register **r2** by the instruction

```
ldr(r2, [r1, 0x14])
```

The sequence

```
movw(r3, 0xf<<12)
bic(r2, r3)
```

clears bits corresponding to pins PD12-PD15. Then the new value for PD12-PD15 is loaded in MCU register **r2** by the sequence:

```
lsl(r0, r0, 12)
orr(r2, r0)
```

Finally, the value in MCU register **r2** is written to register GPIO_ODR by the instruction

```
strh(r2, [r1, 0x14])
```

The above code can easily be adapted to the PYBv1.1 board. Since all pins where the LEDs are attached to belong to port GPIOA, we should determine the base address of port GPIOA of STM32F405xx MCU. According to the datasheet on MCU, the base address of port GPIOA is 0x4002 0000.The address offset of register GPIO_ODR (as well as for any other register) will be the same and equal to 0x14.
That is all what we need to write the code (**Listing 21**) for PYBv1.1.

Listing 21.

```python
from pyb import Pin
pGreen = Pin('A13', Pin.OUT_PP)
pRed = Pin('A14', Pin.OUT_PP)
pOrange = Pin('A15', Pin.OUT_PP)
@micropython.asm_thumb
def write_bits_3(r0):
    movwt(r1, 0x4002<<16)
    ldr(r2, [r1, 0x14])
    movw(r3, 7<<13)
    bic(r2, r3)
    lsl(r0, r0, 13)
    orr(r2, r0)
    strh(r2, [r1, 0x14])
```

To test the above code, simply launch the **write_bits_3()** function with different parameters (0-7) and observe what LED(s) are being affected.

The following two examples also use physical addresses of GPIO to control output pins, but the low-level operations are implemented using register GPIO_BSRR. We already used this register in the previous examples, but now we consider GPIO_BSRR in detail – this helps us to write the effective code using this register.
Register GPIO_BSRR (**Fig.16**) has the address offset 0x18 and provides separate control of digital outputs through low (15-0) and high (31-16) bits.

8.4.7 GPIO port bit set/reset register (GPIOx_BSRR) (x = A..I/J/K)

Address offset: 0x18

Reset value: 0x0000 0000

31	30	29	28	27	26	25	24	23	22	21	20	19	18	17	16
BR15	BR14	BR13	BR12	BR11	BR10	BR9	BR8	BR7	BR6	BR5	BR4	BR3	BR2	BR1	BR0
w	w	w	w	w	w	w	w	w	w	w	w	w	w	w	w
15	14	13	12	11	10	9	8	7	6	5	4	3	2	1	0
BS15	BS14	BS13	BS12	BS11	BS10	BS9	BS8	BS7	BS6	BS5	BS4	BS3	BS2	BS1	BS0
w	w	w	w	w	w	w	w	w	w	w	w	w	w	w	w

Fig.16

In this register, the high bits (31-16), also labeled BR15-BR0, allow to reset (clear) a separate output bit (15-0) in the GPIO_ODR register. These bits are

44

write-only and can be accessed in word, half-word or byte mode. Reading these bits returns the value 0x0000. Writing 0 causes no action on the corresponding GPIO_ODR bit, while writing 1 resets (clears) the corresponding GPIO_ODR bit.

The low bits (15:0) labeled BS15-BS0 allow to set a separate output bit (15-0) in the GPIO_ODR register. These bits are write-only and can be accessed in word, half-word or byte mode. A read to these bits returns the value 0x0000. Writing 0 causes no action on the corresponding GPIO_ODR bit, while writing 1 sets the corresponding GPIO_ODR bit.

If both BSx and BRx are set, BSx has priority.

Using the GPIO_BSRR register to change the values of individual bits in GPIO_ODR is a 'one-shot' effect that does not lock the GPIO_ODR bits. The GPIO_ODR bits can always be accessed directly. The GPIO_BSRR register provides a way of performing atomic bitwise handling.

There is no need for the software to disable interrupts when programming the GPIO_ODR at bit level: it is possible to modify one or more bits in a single atomic AHB1 write access through register GPIO_BSRR.

The **write_bits_4()** function whose code is shown in **Listing 22** allows to control the STM32F407DISCOVERY on-board LEDs through register GPIO_BSRR. As in the previous examples, function **write_bits_4()** takes a single parameter that should range from 0 to 15.

Listing 22.

```
from pyb import Pin
pGreen = Pin('PD12', Pin.OUT_PP)
pOrange = Pin('PD13', Pin.OUT_PP)
pRed = Pin('PD14', Pin.OUT_PP)
pBlue = Pin('PD15', Pin.OUT_PP)
@micropython.asm_thumb
def write_bits_4(r0):
    movwt(r1, 0x4002<<16)
    movw(r2, 0x0c00)
    add(r1, r1, r2)
    movwt(r2, 0xf<<28)
    str(r2, [r1, 0x18])
    lsl(r0, r0, 12)
    str(r0, [r1, 0x18])
```

In this code, the following assembler instructions load the base address of port GPIOD (=0x40020c00) in the MCU register **r1**.

```
movwt(r1, 0x4002<<16)
movw(r2, 0x0c00)
add(r1, r1, r2)
```

Then we clear all required bits (PD12-PD15) by writing the value 0xf into the high word of register GPIO_BSRR (=0x40020c00+0x18) using the sequence

```
movwt(r2, 0xf<<28)
str(r2, [r1, 0x18])
```

Finally, we write the desired combination of bits kept in MCU register **r0** into the low word of register GPIO_BSRR using the following instructions:

```
lsl(r0, r0, 12)
str(r0, [r1, 0x18])
```

To test the above code, simply launch the **write_bits_4()** function with different parameters (0-15) and observe how the LED(s) are affected.

```
write_bits_4(10)
write_bits_4(6)
write_bits_4(0)
write_bits_4(13)
```

The MicroPython code using GPIO_BSRR for control of the PYBv1.1 on-board LEDs is shown in **Listing 23**. Here, function **write_bits_4()** takes a single parameter that should range from 0 to 7.

Listing 23.

```
from pyb import Pin
pGreen = Pin('A13', Pin.OUT_PP)
pRed = Pin('A14', Pin.OUT_PP)
pOrange = Pin('A15', Pin.OUT_PP)
@micropython.asm_thumb
```

```
def write_bits_4(r0):
    movwt(r1, 0x4002<<16)
    movwt(r2, 7<<29)
    str(r2, [r1, 0x18])
    lsl(r0, r0, 13)
    str(r0, [r1, 0x18])
```

In this code, the following assembler instruction loads the base address of port GPIOA (=0x40020000) in MCU register **r1**.

```
movwt(r1, 0x4002<<16)
```

The we clear all required bits (PD12-PD15) by writing the value 0xf into the high word of register GPIO_BSRR (=0x40020000+0x18) using the sequence

```
movwt(r2, 7<<29)
str(r2, [r1, 0x18])
```

Finally, we write the desired combination of bits kept in MCU register **r0** into the low word of register GPIO_BSRR using the following instructions:

```
lsl(r0, r0, 13)
str(r0, [r1, 0x18])
```

To test the above code, simply launch the **write_bits_4()** function with different parameters (0-15) and observe how the LED(s) are affected.

```
write_bits_4(1)
write_bits_4(6)
write_bits_4(0)
write_bits_4(7)
```

Low-level programming digital inputs

This section describes programming techniques for reading data from digital inputs. Here we will consider step by step how to process a signal from a single input on PYBv1.1. This board has the USR button attached to pin

PB4 – we will use this peripheral to illustrate the basic approaches while processing digital input signals.

The following sequence configures pin PB4 as a digital input without pull-up/pull-down resistors:

```
machine.mem32[stm.GPIOB + stm.GPIO_MODER] &= ~(3<<6)
machine.mem32[stm.GPIOB + stm.GPIO_PUPDR] &= ~(3<<6)
```

Note that the proper selection of a pull-up/pull-down option depends on external circuitry connected to the input pin. Be very careful when using the same pin as input and output (in my opinion, that's a bad idea). In this case, think carefully about protecting an output against current overflow.

Once configuration is complete, we can read the data from input PB4 by the statement:

```
print((machine.mem32[stm.GPIOB + stm.GPIO_IDR] & 0x8) >> 3)
```

This statement displays the value read from input PB4 on the screen. For PYBv1.1, the released USR button provides a high voltage level (=log.'1') on the PB4 input, while the pressed button provides a low voltage level (=log.'0').

The following code (**Listing 24**) allows to read input PB4 every 2 s.

Listing 24.

```
import time
machine.mem32[stm.GPIOB + stm.GPIO_MODER] &= ~(3<<6)
machine.mem32[stm.GPIOB + stm.GPIO_PUPDR] &= ~(3<<6)
inpState = True
while True:
    inpState = bool((machine.mem16[stm.GPIOB + \
    stm.GPIO_IDR] & 0x8) >> 3)
    print(inpState)
    time.sleep(2)
```

The application produces either **True** or **False** depending on the state of the pin PB4. When the USR button is pressed, the application returns **False** (log.'0'). Conversely, when the button is released, the application returns **True** (log.'1').

To write faster code, we can rewrite the function reading digital input in the inline assembler (**Listing 25**). In this code, function **read_pin()** returns either 0 or 1 depending on the state of the PB4 input.

Listing 25.

```
import time
machine.mem32[stm.GPIOB + stm.GPIO_MODER] &= ~(3<<6)
machine.mem32[stm.GPIOB + stm.GPIO_PUPDR] &= ~(3<<6)
@micropython.asm_thumb
def read_pin():
    movwt(r0, stm.GPIOB)
    ldr(r0, [r0, stm.GPIO_IDR])
    lsr(r0, r0, 3)
    movwt(r1, 0xFFFFFFFE)
    bic(r0, r1)
inpState = True
while True:
    inpState = bool(read_pin())
    print(inpState)
    time.sleep(2)
```

The application produces the True (log.'1') output when the user button is released and False (log.'0') when the button is pressed.

Note that similar programming techniques can be applied to other boards capable of running MicroPython and equipped with STM32F405/407 MCU.

Parallel processing several input pins

Reading digital inputs in parallel will be useful while fast evaluating signals from several sensors at a time.

To illustrate programming techniques applied to implementing such a task, the following simple circuit (**Fig.17**) was assembled. In this circuit, two switches are connected to pins PC6 ("Y1") and PC7("Y2") of PYBv1.1.

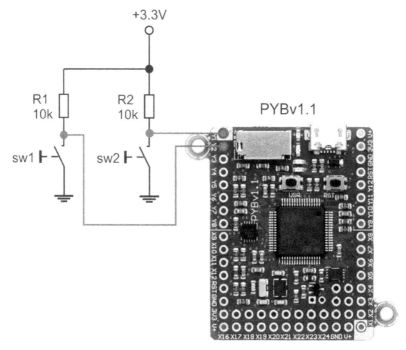

Fig.17

Pins PC6 and PC7 correspond to bits 6 and 7 of port GPIOC. Before reading data from these pins, configure them as digital inputs without pull-up/pull-down. That is done by the following statements:

machine.mem32[stm.GPIOC + stm.GPIO_MODER] &= ~(0x33<<12)
machine.mem32[stm.GPIOC + stm.GPIO_PUPDR] &= ~(0x33<<12)

Now the state of pins PC6-PC7 will be read through bits 6-7 of register GPIO_IDR. For convenience, let's assume that bits PC6 and PC7 will be interpreted as 'bit 0' and 'bit 1', respectively. All possible combinations of these bits are shown in the **Table 5**.

Table 5. Possible states of input pins PC6 and PC7

State of Pin C6 (bit 0)	State of Pin C7 (bit 1)	Binary Code
Released (bit 0 = 1)	Released (bit 1 = 1)	0b11
Pressed (bit 0 = 0)	Released (bit 1 = 1)	0b10
Released (bit 0 = 1)	Pressed (bit 1 = 0)	0b01

| Pressed (bit 0 = 0) | Pressed (bit 1 = 0) | 0b00 |

To display the state of pin PC6-PC7 on the screen, we can use the following statement:

print(bin((machine.mem16[stm.GPIOC + stm.GPIO_IDR] & 0xC0) >> 6))

Fast processing several inputs at a time requires an inline assembler. The low-level code that configures pins PC6-PC7 as inputs is placed in function **config_pins()** as is shown in **Listing 26**.

Listing 26.

```
@micropython.asm_thumb
def config_pins():
    movwt(r0, stm.GPIOC)
    ldr(r1, [r0, stm.GPIO_MODER])
    movwt(r2, 0x33<<12)
    bic(r1, r2)
    str(r1, [r0, stm.GPIO_MODER])
    ldr(r1, [r0, stm.GPIO_PUPDR])
    bic(r1, r2)
    str(r1, [r0, stm.GPIO_PUPDR])
```

Function **read_pins()** whose code is shown in **Listing 27** allows to read data on pins PC6-PC7 at a time.

Listing 27.

```
@micropython.asm_thumb
def read_pins():
    movwt(r0, stm.GPIOC)
    ldr(r0, [r0, stm.GPIO_IDR])
    lsr(r0, r0, 6)
    movwt(r1, 0xFFFFFFFC)
    bic(r0,r1)
```

With the **config_pins()** and **read_pins()** functions, reading pins PC6-PC7 may be implemented as follows:

```
. . . . . .
import time
config_pins()
while True:
    print(bin(read_pins()))
    time.sleep(1)
. . . . . .
```

Let's consider one more example. Assume that the MicroPython code should drive the on-board LED ON only when both switches connected to pins PC6-PC7 are pressed (=0). Also assume that any other combination of input signals causes the LED to be driven OFF.
The MicroPytnon code implementing such algorithm is shown in **Listing 28**.

Listing 28.

```
from pyb import LED
import time
@micropython.asm_thumb
def config_pins():
    movwt(r0, stm.GPIOC)
    ldr(r1, [r0, stm.GPIO_MODER])
    movwt(r2, 0x33<<12)
    bic(r1, r2)
    str(r1, [r0, stm.GPIO_MODER])
    ldr(r1, [r0, stm.GPIO_PUPDR])
    bic(r1, r2)
    str(r1, [r0, stm.GPIO_PUPDR])
@micropython.asm_thumb
def read_pins():
    movwt(r0, stm.GPIOC)
    ldr(r0, [r0, stm.GPIO_IDR])
    lsr(r0, r0, 6)
    movwt(r1, 0xFFFFFFFC)
    bic(r0,r1)
led = LED(1)
config_pins()
while True:
    if read_pins() == 0x0:
        led.on()
```

```
else:
    led.off()
time.sleep_ms(100)
```

We can periodically read input pins without blocking the rest of code by using some MCU timer. In that case, the read operation on input pins will be executed within an Interrupt Service Routine (ISR) being invoked when the timer overflows.

The following example (**Listing 29**) illustrates using Timer 2 for polling inputs PC6-PC7 every 100 mS (milliseconds). The foreground code doesn't waste time on reading inputs, it simply reads the state of both inputs stored in variable **pinState**.

Listing 29.

```
from pyb import LED, Timer
import time
pinState = 0
@micropython.asm_thumb
def config_pins():
    movwt(r0, stm.GPIOC)
    ldr(r1, [r0, stm.GPIO_MODER])
    movwt(r2, 0x33<<12)
    bic(r1, r2)
    str(r1, [r0, stm.GPIO_MODER])
    ldr(r1, [r0, stm.GPIO_PUPDR])
    bic(r1, r2)
    str(r1, [r0, stm.GPIO_PUPDR])
@micropython.asm_thumb
def read_pins():
    movwt(r0, stm.GPIOC)
    ldr(r0, [r0, stm.GPIO_IDR])
    lsr(r0, r0, 6)
    movwt(r1, 0xfffffffc)
    bic(r0,r1)
def tim2_isr(timer):
    global pinState
    pinState = read_pins()
tim2 = Timer(2, freq=10)
tim2.callback(tim2_isr)
```

```
while True:
    print(bin(pinState))
    <do something>
    . . . . . . .
```

Programming external interrupts

On suitable hardware MicroPython offers the ability to write interrupt handlers. Interrupt handlers – also known as Interrupt Service Routines (ISR's) – are defined as callback functions. These are executed in response to an event such as a timer trigger or a voltage change on a pin. Such events can occur at any point in the execution of the program code.

Acceptable code size of an ISR are dependent on the rate at which interrupts occur, the nature of the main program, and the presence of other concurrent events. The practical recommendations on writing ISR code are detailed in MicroPython documentation.

In practice, writing fast ISR code in MicroPython is a complicated task. It is a common requirement that the code of ISR should be as short as possible. Also the ISR code should be fast. Both requirement may be achieved either by using the functions from the **machine** module or inline assembler instructions.

The first example (**Listing 30**) illustrates using low-level instructions from the **machine** module to increase the performance an application where an external interrupt should be processed.

Listing 30.

```
from pyb import Pin, ExtInt
import array
from uctypes import addressof

cnt = array.array('i', [0])
pcnt = addressof(cnt)
pRed = Pin('A14', Pin.OUT_PP)
def ext1_isr(param):
    global pcnt
    machine.mem32[pcnt] += 1
ext1 = ExtInt(Pin('Y1'), ExtInt.IRQ_RISING, Pin.PULL_NONE, ext1_isr)
```

```
while True:
    if cnt[0] > 9:
        machine.mem32[pcnt] = 0
        machine.mem32[stm.GPIOA + stm.GPIO_ODR] ^= 0b1 << 14
```

In this code, the Red LED (pin PA14 on the PYBv1.1) is toggled after 10
transitions '0-1' on pin PC6 ('Y1') occur.
To achieve maximum performance, we use only a single low-level function
within an ISR:

```
machine.mem32[pcnt] += 1
```

This function simply increments the counter **cnt[0]** each time the rising edge
arrives on pin PC6. To fast access to **cnt[0]**, the function uses the pointer
pcnt to the counter.
Additionally, to optimize the overall performance, we use low-level functions
in the **while True** loop. Since pin PA14 is already configured in the
initialization section of code, we gain direct control over the LED through
register GPIO_ODR.

The second example (**Listing 31**) illustrates using a MicroPython inline
assembler in ISR. In this application, the external interrupt will be triggered
on either rising or falling edge on pin 'Y1' (bit 6 of port GPIOC).
The Interrupt Service Routine when called gains control over bits PA13
(Green LED) and PA14 (Red LED) of port GPIOA.
When a falling edge is detected, the Green LED is ON (bit PA13 is set) and
Red LED is OFF (bit PA14 is clear).
When a rising edge is detected, the Green LED is OFF (bit PA13 is clear)
and Red LED is ON (bit PA14 of is set).

Listing 31.

```
from pyb import Pin, ExtInt
pGreen = Pin('A13', Pin.OUT_PP)
pRed = Pin('A14', Pin.OUT_PP)
@micropython.asm_thumb
def ext1_isr(r0):
    push({r0, r1, r2})
    movwt(r0, stm.GPIOC)
    ldr(r1, [r0, stm.GPIO_IDR])
```

```
movw(r2, 1<<6)
and_(r1, r2)
mov(r2, r1)
movwt(r0, stm.GPIOA)
ldr(r1, [r0, stm.GPIO_ODR])
eor(r1, r1)
str(r1, [r0, stm.GPIO_ODR])
cmp(r2, 0)
beq(set_green)
b(set_red)
label(set_green)
movw(r1, 1<<13)
b(exit)
label(set_red)
movw(r1, 1<<14)
label(exit)
str(r1, [r0, stm.GPIO_ODR])
pop({r0, r1, r2})
ext1 = ExtInt(Pin('Y1'), ExtInt.IRQ_RISING_FALLING, \
Pin.PULL_NONE, ext1_isr)
```

Note that if we use an inline assembler within the ISR code, we must place (push) all MCU registers being affected onto the stack by the **push()** instruction before any other instruction begins to run. When ISR code returns control to the main loop, these register must be restored (popped) from the stack by the **pop()** instruction. The system throws the exception if we forget to save / restore the registers affected by ISR code.
In our case, we place the MCU registers **r0 – r2** onto the stack by the first instruction in ISR code:

```
push({r0, r1, r2})
```

and restore them by the last instruction

```
pop({r0, r1, r2})
```

The following sequence

```
movwt(r0, stm.GPIOC)
ldr(r1, [r0, stm.GPIO_IDR])
```

```
movw(r2, 1<<6)
and_(r1, r2)
mov(r2, r1)
```

reads bit 6 of port GPIOC (pin 'Y1') and saves its value in MCU register **r2**. Then the code clears all bits in the output data register GPIO_ODR by the sequence

```
movwt(r0, stm.GPIOA)
ldr(r1, [r0, stm.GPIO_ODR])
eor(r1, r1)
str(r1, [r0, stm.GPIO_ODR])
```

After that the following sequence evaluates the value saved in register **r2** (the state of pin 'Y1') and, depending on the result, passes the control to the corresponding branch:

```
cmp(r2, 0)
beq(set_green)
b(set_red)
```

The sequence

```
label(set_green)
movw(r1, 1<<13)
b(exit)
```

sets bit PA13 in register **r1**. The position of this bit corresponds to the Green LED. The last instruction in this section branches to the label **exit**.

Similarly, the section

```
label(set_red)
movw(r1, 1<<14)
```

sets bit PA14 in register **r1**. The position of this bit corresponds to the Red LED.
The last section of the code (label **exit**) contains the following instructions:

```
str(r1, [r0, stm.GPIO_ODR])
```

pop({r0, r1, r2})

The **str()** instruction writes the updated value in the data register GPIO_ODR of port GPIOA. The code ends with the **pop()** instruction that restores the contents of the CPU registers **r0 – r2** from the stack.

Optimizing ISR code

If we want to maximize the speed of low-level code, the following simple rules may come in handy:

- avoid subsequent function calls within the ISR code, since such calls require additional operations on the stack thus decreasing overall performance;
- the branches within the ISR code slow down the performance, therefore try to eliminate branches (if possible) or, at least, reduce their number. This is especially important for the ISR code that should run as fast as possible.

To eliminate extra branches, we can use the low-level implementation of If-Then block for Cortex-M4 MCU called **it()**. The Thumb-2 implementation of the **it()** instruction makes up to four following instructions conditional. The conditions can be all the same, or some of them can be the logical inverse of the others.

Let's make the optimization of the code from **Listing 31** by using the **it()** assembler instruction in the ISR code (function **ext1_isr**).

The optimized version of the code for PYBv1.1 is shown in **Listing 32**.

Listing 32.

```
from pyb import Pin, ExtInt
pGreen = Pin('A13', Pin.OUT_PP)
pRed = Pin('A14', Pin.OUT_PP)
@micropython.asm_thumb
def ext1_isr(r0):
    push({r0, r1, r2})
    movwt(r0, stm.GPIOC)
    ldr(r1, [r0, stm.GPIO_IDR])
    movw(r2, 1<<6)
```

```
    and_(r1, r2)
    mov(r2, r1)
    movwt(r0, stm.GPIOA)
    ldr(r1, [r0, stm.GPIO_ODR])
    eor(r1, r1)
    str(r1, [r0, stm.GPIO_ODR])
    cmp(r2, 0)
    ite(eq)
    movw(r1, 1<<13)
    movw(r1, 1<<14)
    str(r1, [r0, stm.GPIO_ODR])
    pop({r0, r1, r2})
ext1 = ExtInt(Pin('Y1'), ExtInt.IRQ_RISING_FALLING, \
Pin.PULL_NONE, ext1_sr)
```

In this code, using the **ite(eq)** conditional instruction allows to completely eliminate the branches present in the earlier version of this code. More precisely, the block of instructions

```
beq(set_green)
b(set_red)
label(set_green)
movw(r1, 1<<13)
b(exit)
label(set_red)
movw(r1, 1<<14)
label(exit)
str(r1, [r0, stm.GPIO_ODR])
```

has been replaced with the following one

```
ite(eq)
movw(r1, 1<<13)
movw(r1, 1<<14)
str(r1, [r0, stm.GPIO_ODR])
```

The following MicroPython code that implements the similar algorithm but for STM32F407DISCOVERY is shown in **Listing 33**.

In this application, the external interrupt is triggered on pin PC0. The ISR code controls Green LED (pin PD12) and Red LED (pin PD14).

Listing 33.

```
from pyb import Pin, ExtInt
pGreen = Pin('PD12', Pin.OUT_PP)
pRed = Pin('PD14', Pin.OUT_PP)
@micropython.asm_thumb
def write_pins():
    push({r0, r1, r2})
    movwt(r0, stm.GPIOC)
    ldr(r1, [r0, stm.GPIO_IDR])
    movw(r2, 1)
    and_(r1, r2)
    mov(r2, r1)
    movwt(r0, stm.GPIOD)
    ldr(r1, [r0, stm.GPIO_ODR])
    eor(r1, r1)
    str(r1, [r0, stm.GPIO_ODR])
    cmp(r2, 0)
    ite(eq)
    movw(r1, 1<<12)
    movw(r1, 1<<14)
    str(r1, [r0, stm.GPIO_ODR])
    pop({r0, r1, r2})
def ext1_isr(param):
    write_pins()
ext1 = ExtInt(Pin('PC0'), ExtInt.IRQ_RISING_FALLING, \
Pin.PULL_NONE, ext1_isr)
```

External interrupts in measurement applications

One of useful applications where external interrupts come in handy is to detect a single pulse (tick) passed through a digital input. In this case, we are only interested in knowing that a single pulse passed. To detect the pulse, we can use a counter **cnt** being incremented until it reaches 2. When this happens, we consider that a single pulse passed. This case is illustrated in **Fig.18**.

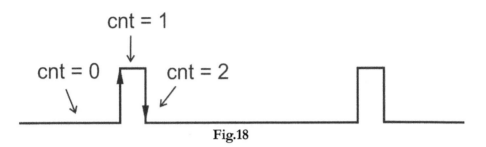

Fig.18

The MicroPython code shown in **Listing 34** allows to detect pulses arriving on pin PC6 ('Y1') of PYBv1.1. To clarify the algorithm, the ISR code is written using high-level statements, although in real-time applications we should apply low-level instructions.

Listing 34.

```
from pyb import Pin, ExtInt
import time
def ext1_isr(param):
    global cnt
    if cnt == 2:
        return
    elif cnt == 1:
        cnt += 1
        return
    else:
        if machine.mem32[stm.GPIOC + stm.GPIO_IDR] & 0x40 != 0:
            cnt = 1
cnt = 0
ext1 = ExtInt(Pin('Y1'), ExtInt.IRQ_RISING_FALLING, \
Pin.PULL_NONE, ext1_isr)
while True:
    if cnt == 2:
        print("Pulse detected.")
        cnt = 0
```

One more implementation of this algorithm is shown in **Listing 35**. In this application, the ISR code is written in an inline assembler thus providing more compact code and better performance.

Listing 35.

```python
from pyb import Pin, ExtInt
import array
from uctypes import addressof
cnt = array.array('i', [0])
pcnt = addressof(cnt)
@micropython.asm_thumb
def get_cnt(r0):
    push({r0, r1, r2, r3})
    ldr(r1, [r0, 0])
    cmp(r1, 2)
    beq(exit)
    cmp(r1, 1)
    ittt(eq)
    add(r1,r1,1)
    str(r1, [r0, 0])
    b(exit)
    movwt(r2, stm.GPIOC)
    ldr(r3, [r2, stm.GPIO_IDR])
    cmp(r1, 0)
    itt(eq)
    lsr(r3, r3, 7)
    bcs(set_1)
    b(exit)
    label(set_1)
    movw(r1, 1)
    str(r1, [r0, 0])
    label(exit)
    pop({r0, r1, r2, r3})
def ext1_isr(param):
    global pcnt
    get_cnt(pcnt)
ext1 = ExtInt(Pin('Y1'), ExtInt.IRQ_RISING_FALLING, \
Pin.PULL_NONE, ext1_isr)
while True:
    if cnt[0] == 2:
        print("Pulse detected.")
        cnt[0] = 0
```

The main job in this code is performed by function **get_cnt()** that takes a single parameter. For maximum performance, this function will access the counter **cnt** through its address in memory (pointer **pcnt**).

With external interrupts, it is easily to calculate the number of pulses captured on a digital input during some interval. In the case of a pulse train, we get the frequency (period) of a signal by counting the rising (falling) edges (**Fig.19**).

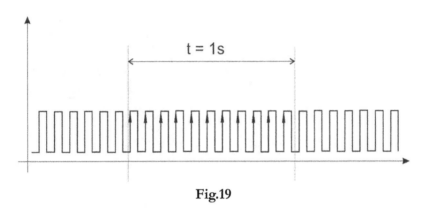

Fig.19

The following application allows to count the number of rising edges arriving on pin PC6('Y1') of PYBv1.1 during 1 s (**Fig.20**). This number gives us the frequency of a signal in Hz.

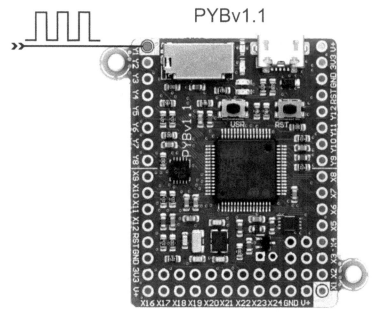

Fig.20

The above circuit was tested at the input frequencies in the range of 12 Hz to 50 KHz. The test signal source provided the push-pull output, while the 'Y1' input of PYBv1.1 was configured as PULL_NONE.

The MicroPython code for this application is shown in **Listing 36**.

Listing 36.

```
from pyb import Pin, ExtInt
import time
def ext1_isr(param):
    global cnt
    cnt += 1
cnt = 0
ext1 = ExtInt(Pin('Y1'), ExtInt.IRQ_RISING, \
Pin.PULL_NONE, ext1_isr)
while True:
    cnt = 0
    time.sleep(1)
    print(cnt)
```

```
        time.sleep(5)
```

The application works as follows. Each time the interrupt **ext1** is triggered by the rising edge, the **ext1_isr** code increments the counter (variable **cnt**). At the beginning of each iteration, the code within the **while True** loop clears **cnt**, then waits 1 s. After 1s interval expires, the **cnt** variable will hold the value equal to the frequency of an input pulse train. The measurements repeat every 5 s.

Despite its simplicity, the above code provides very high precision while measuring the frequency in the range of 12 Hz – 50 KHz. For the input frequency of 50KHz, the error achieves 3-5 Hz. At higher input frequencies (>50 KHz), the precision of measurements will degrade due to hardware/software limitations.

To reach more performance, we can rewrite the above example using an inline assembler (**Listing 37**).

Listing 37.

```
from pyb import Pin, ExtInt
import array
from uctypes import addressof
import time
@micropython.asm_thumb
def inc_cnt(r0):
    push ({r1, r2})
    ldr(r1, [r0, 0])
    movw(r2, 1)
    add(r1, r1, r2)
    str(r1, [r0, 0])
    pop({r1, r2})
cnt = array.array('i', [0])
pcnt = addressof(cnt)
def int_isr(param):
    global pcnt
    inc_cnt(pcnt)
ext1 = ExtInt(Pin('Y1'), ExtInt.IRQ_RISING, \
Pin.PULL_NONE, int_isr)
while True:
```

```
cnt[0] = 0
time.sleep(1)
print(cnt[0])
time.sleep(7)
```

With this code, the upper limit of high precision measurements achieves 62.5KHz (period = 16 uS).

Using external interrupts, it is possible to measure the pulse width of a rectangular pulse arriving on a digital input. This may be performed by measuring the interval between rising and falling edges of a pulse. The following example code (**Listing 38**) allows to make high precision measurement of a pulse width.

Listing 38.

```
from pyb import Pin, ExtInt
import time
edge = 0
start = 0
delta = 0
@micropython.asm_thumb
def get_input():
    movwt(r0, stm.GPIOC)
    ldr(r1, [r0, stm.GPIO_IDR])
    movw(r2, 1<<6)
    and_(r1, r2)
    lsr(r1, r1, 6)
    mov(r0, r1)
def ext1_isr(param):
    global edge
    edge = get_input()
ext1 = ExtInt(Pin('Y1'), ExtInt.IRQ_RISING_FALLING, \
Pin.PULL_NONE, ext1_isr)
while True:
    while edge == 1: continue
    while edge == 0: continue
    start = time.ticks_us()
    while edge == 1: continue
    delta = time.ticks_diff(time.ticks_us(), start)
```

```
print(delta)
time.sleep(7)
```

In this code, variable **delta** holds the result of measurements. This application exhibits the error of 6-8 µS in the range of $20 - 1200$ µS. The following MicroPython code (**Listing 39**) is a bit faster than previous one from **Listing 38**.

Listing 39.

```
from pyb import Pin, ExtInt
from uctypes import addressof
import time
import array
edge = array.array('i', [0])
p_edge = addressof(edge)
start = 0
delta = 0
@micropython.asm_thumb
def get_input(r0):
    movwt(r1, stm.GPIOC)
    ldr(r2, [r1, stm.GPIO_IDR])
    movw(r3, 1<<6)
    and_(r2, r3)
    str(r2, [r0, 0])
def ext1_isr(param):
    global p_edge
    get_input(p_edge)
ext1 = ExtInt(Pin('Y1'), ExtInt.IRQ_RISING_FALLING, \
Pin.PULL_NONE, ext1_isr)
while True:
    while edge[0] > 0: continue
    while edge[0] == 0: continue
    start = time.ticks_us()
    while edge[0] > 0: continue
    delta = time.ticks_diff(time.ticks_us(), start)
    print(delta)
    time.sleep(7)
```

With this code, the precision of the pulse width measurements reaches 5-7µS in the range of $35 - 120$ µS and 3-4 µS for pulse widths > 120 µS.

Timing in MicroPython Applications

This section discusses timing operations in MicroPython applications and practical examples running on PYBv1.1 and STM32F4DISCOVERY boards. All tasks that should perform some timing operations usually involve MCU timers. Timers provides numerous capabilities to ease the development of effective timing algorithms. In this section, we will consider various examples of using timers in various MicroPython applications.

Timers in loops and delays

In MicroPython applications, timers come in handy when we need to implement precision time-dependent loops and delays. The example code in **Listing 40** illustrates a simple method of implementing a periodic task synchronized by a timer.

Listing 40.

```
from pyb import Pin, Timer
p_out = Pin('Y1', Pin.OUT_PP)
cnt = 0
def tim1_isr(timer):
    global cnt
    cnt += 1
tim1 = Timer(1, freq=10000)
tim1.callback(tim1_isr)
while True:
    if cnt > 9:
        p_out.value(not p_out.value())
        cnt = 0
    . . .
    <do something>
    . . .
```

This code written for PYBv1.1 toggles the output pin (variable **p_out**) every 1 millisecond (mS). The interval is determined by both Timer 1 (variable **tim1**) and variable **cnt**.

Timer 1 is configured to overflow every 100 microseconds (μS) that corresponds to the frequency of 10.0KHz. The code within the **while True** loop checks **cnt** within the **if()** statement. When **cnt** reaches 10, the output **p_out** toggles. This occurs every

cnt x 100 = 10 x 100 μS = 1 mS

In fact, the **if()** construction implements a non-blocking delay, allowing the rest of code to immediately execute if the condition (**cnt < 9**) is false.

To achieve the maximum performance of code, it is reasonable to make the Interrupt Service Routine (ISR) as short as possible. Therefore, the code within the ISR **tim1_isr** does nothing but simply increments variable **cnt**.

With the above code, it is possible to execute periodic tasks capable of running very long time. This can be achieved by configuring Timer 1 and/or setting the desired threshold for the **cnt** variable.

For relatively short intervals, we can exclude the **cnt** variable from the code as is illustrated in **Listing 41**.

Listing 41.

```
from pyb import Pin, Timer
p_out = Pin('Y1', Pin.OUT_PP)
flag = 0
def tim1_isr(timer):
    global flag
    flag = 1
tim1 = Timer(1, freq=20000)
tim1.callback(tim1_isr)
while True:
    if flag == 1:
        p_out.value(not p_out.value())
        flag = 0
    . . .
    <do something>
    . . .
```

In this example, Timer 1 (variable **tim1**) operates at the frequency of 20000 Hz that corresponds to the period of 50 μS between successive interrupts. With this period, the code within the **if()** statement in the **while True** loop toggles pin 'Y1' (variable **p_out**). The code within the **tim1_isr** ISR simply sets the **flag** variable thus enabling the code within the **if()** statement to run. Again, as in the previous example, the **if()** statement doesn't block the rest of code.

If our task should perform the single I/O operation on a pin, we can put the fragment of code implementing this task in an ISR. This case is illustrated in **Listing 42**.

Listing 42.

```
from pyb import Pin, Timer
p_out = Pin('Y1', Pin.OUT_PP)
def tim1_isr(timer):
    global p_out
    p_out.value(not p_out.value())
tim1 = Timer(1, freq=20000)
tim1.callback(tim1_isr)
. . .
<do something>
. . .
```

To make the above code a bit faster, we can rewrite the ISR (callback function) using the inline assembler (**Listing 43**).

Listing 43.

```
from pyb import Pin, Timer
p_out = Pin('Y1', Pin.OUT_PP)
@micropython.asm_thumb
def tim1_isr(r0):
    push({r0, r1, r2})
    movwt(r0, stm.GPIOC)
    ldr(r1, [r0, stm.GPIO_ODR])
    movw(r2, 1<<6)
    eor(r1, r2)
    str(r1, [r0, stm.GPIO_ODR])
```

```
     pop({r0, r1, r2})
tim1 = Timer(1, freq=20000)
tim1.callback(tim1_isr)
```

In this code, we use register GPIO_ODR of port GPIOC to toggle bit PC6 (pin 'Y1'). **Note** that we must store the registers affected by the ISR code on the stack by the instruction

```
push({r0, r1, r2})
```

at the beginning of code.
When ISR code terminates, we must restore the same registers by the statement

```
pop({r0, r1, r2})
```

that must be the last instruction in our code.
One approach to implement a high-precision non-blocking delay is to directly use the counter of a timer. In this case, the frequency of the clock source feeding the counter can be selected reasonably high.
The following code (**Listing 44**) illustrates this approach. In this code, the LED(1) of PYBv1.1 will be toggled every 1s.

Listing 44.

```
from pyb import LED, Timer
led = LED(1)
tim2 = Timer(2, prescaler=83, period=0x3fffffff)
tim2.counter(0)
while True:
    if tim2.counter() > 1000000:
        led.toggle()
        tim2.counter(0)
```

In this code, the counter of Timer 2 (variable **tim2**) is fed by the frequency of 1MHz whose value is defined by Prescaler (=83). For PYBv1.1, the clock source for timers provides the frequency of 84 MHz, therefore the frequency F feeding the counter will be calculated as follows:

$$F = 84 \text{ MHz} / (\text{Prescaler}+1) = 84 \text{ MHz} / 84 = 1 \text{ MHz}$$

Consequently, period T between two successive ticks is

$$T = 1 / F = 1 \; \mu S$$

Since we need a delay of 1 s = 1000000 μS, our code should detect when 1000000 ticks have passed. It is convenient to start counting from 0, therefore each delay is started by clearing the counter.

One more example code (**Listing 45**) providing high-precision delays is based upon using a real-time clock (RTC).

Listing 45.

```
from pyb import Pin, LED, RTC
import time
led = LED(4)
pa8 = Pin('A8', Pin.OUT_PP)
callback = lambda p: pyb.Pin('A8').high()
rtc1 = RTC()
cnt = 0
pa8.low()
rtc1.wakeup(1000, callback)
while True:
    if pa8.value() == 1:
        led.toggle()
        pa8.low()
        rtc1.wakeup(1000, callback)
        cnt += 1
        print(cnt)
    time.sleep(0.7)
```

In this code, the Blue LED of PYBv1.1 is toggled every 1 s after RTC time-out is triggered. Here pin PA8 (variable **pa8**) is used as a flag that is set each time when the RTC time-out is triggered. Again, using the **if()** structure allows non-blocking operations.
When choosing the frequency of RTC, notice that the reading / writing operations on a digital pin require some time. Therefore, the interval between two successive interrupts should be more than enough to complete reading / writing operation(s) before the next interrupt is triggered. Also notice that

the performance of foreground code running in the main loop can degrade when external interrupts occurs too often.

For that reason, if your timer must operate at a high frequency, for example, 1 MHz (the period between interrupts = 1μS), the ISR code should be highly optimized to provide fast response.

Often we need to perform some task only once after some predetermined interval expires. Such a task can be implemented using a timer configured to operate in compare match mode as is illustrated in the example for PYBv1.1 (**Listing 46**). In this code, Timer 2 sets (=1) the digital output pin PA5 associated with Channel 1 when 10 s interval expires.

Listing 46.

```
from pyb import Pin, Timer
p_comp = Pin('A5')
tim2 = Timer(2, prescaler=83, period=0x3fffffff)
ch1 = tim2.channel(1, Timer.OC_ACTIVE, compare=10000000, \
polarity=Timer.HIGH, pin=p_comp)
```

In this code, Channel 1 of Timer 2 is configured to operate in OC_ACTIVE mode. In this mode, the output pin will be made active when a compare match occurs. The active state of pin is determined by the parameter **polarity** that, in our case, is assigned Timer.HIGH. This means that when 10 s interval expires, the output pin PA5 corresponding to Channel 1 goes HIGH (=1).

Note that in this state the output pin will stay until the program code clears PA5 by one of the following ways.

One way is to put the output in inactive state by reconfiguring Channel 1 as follows:

```
ch1 = tim2.channel(1, Timer.OC_FORCED_INACTIVE, pin=p_comp)
```

Note that the above statement only affects the output pin itself, while the counter of Timer 2 is kept running.

One more important thing to remember: once the timer operates in OC_FORCED_INACTIVE or OC_FORCED_ACTIVE mode, the timing for the output pin doesn't work! To regain control of the output pin, we must put Timer 2 in OC_ACTIVE mode again by the statement

```
ch1 = tim2.channel(1, Timer.OC_ACTIVE, compare=10000000, \
polarity=Timer.HIGH, pin=p_comp)
```

The next example (**Listing 47**) illustrates switching an output pin from inactive to active state.

Listing 47.

```
ch1 = tim2.channel(1, Timer.OC_FORCED_INACTIVE, pin=p_comp)
ch1 = tim2.channel(1, Timer.OC_ACTIVE, compare=10000000, \
polarity=Timer.HIGH, pin=p_comp)
tim2.counter(0)
```

One more example (**Listing 48**) illustrates toggling pin PA15:

Listing 48.

```
ch1 = tim2.channel(1, Timer.OC_FORCED_INACTIVE, pin=p_comp)
ch1 = tim2.channel(1, Timer.OC_FORCED_ACTIVE, pin=p_comp)
ch1 = tim2.channel(1, Timer.OC_FORCED_INACTIVE, pin=p_comp)
ch1 = tim2.channel(1, Timer.OC_FORCED_ACTIVE, pin=p_comp)
```

The fast code snippets for setting/clearing output pin associated with some timer channel is shown below.
Writing the value 0b100 directly into OC1M[2:0] bits in the capture/compare mode register TIM_CCMR1 by the statement

```
machine.mem32[stm.TIM2 + stm.TIM_CCMR1] = 0b100 << 4
```

forces the compare output PA5 to go inactive (LOW, in our case). Conversely, the statement

```
machine.mem32[stm.TIM2 + stm.TIM_CCMR1] = 0b101 << 4
```

forces the compare output PA5 to go active (HIGH, in our case).
To put Timer 2 in OC_ACTIVE mode, we can also use the low-level function

```
machine.mem32[stm.TIM2 + stm.TIM_CCMR1] = 0b001 << 4
```

This instruction simply writes the code 0b001 into bits OC1M[2:0] of the capture/compare register TIM_CCMR1 – this puts timer 2 in OC_ACTIVE mode.

The following demo application toggles the LED attached to pin PA0 ('X1') of PYBv1.1 (**Fig.21**).

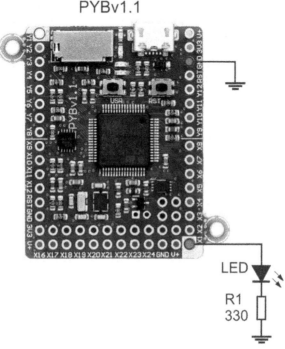

Fig.21

This demo code (**Listing 49**) performs the delay of 10 s before the output PA0 is driven in active state (HIGH). To do that, we configure Channel 1 of 32-bit Timer 5 to operate in OC_ACTIVE mode. After PA0 has been set, the code waits 1 s, then pin PA0 is driven in inactive state (LOW) and the loop repeats.

Listing 49.

```
from pyb import Pin, Timer
p_comp = Pin('A0')
tim5 = Timer(5, prescaler=83, period=0x3fffffff)
```

```
ch1 = tim5.channel(1, Timer.OC_ACTIVE, compare=10000000,\
polarity=Timer.HIGH, pin=p_comp)
while True:
    machine.mem32[stm.TIM5 + stm.TIM_CR1] &= 0xfffe
    machine.mem32[stm.TIM5 + stm.TIM_CCMR1] = 0b100 << 4
    machine.mem32[stm.TIM5 + stm.TIM_CCMR1] = 0b001 << 4
    machine.mem32[stm.TIM5 + stm.TIM_CNT] = 0x0
    machine.mem32[stm.TIM5 + stm.TIM_CR1]  |= 0x1
    while tim5.counter() < 11000000: continue
```

In this code, each iteration begins with the statement

machine.mem32[stm.TIM5 + stm.TIM_CR1] &= 0xfffe

that stops the counter of Timer 5.

Then the code puts Channel 1 of Timer 5 in OC_FORCED_INACTIVE mode by the statement

machine.mem32[stm.TIM5 + stm.TIM_CCMR1] = 0b100 << 4

This causes pin PA0 to be brought in inactive state (LED is OFF). Then the statement

machine.mem32[stm.TIM5 + stm.TIM_CCMR1] = 0b001 << 4

puts Channel 1 of Timer 5 in OC_ACTIVE mode. The last preparation step is to clear the counter of Timer 5 by the statement:

machine.mem32[stm.TIM5 + stm.TIM_CNT] = 0x0

Then we start Timer 5 by the statement:

machine.mem32[stm.TIM5 + stm.TIM_CR1] |= 0x1

The statement

while tim5.counter() < 11000000: continue

performs the delay of 10 s (= 10000000 µS) before pin PA0 is driven to active state (LED is ON) plus the additional delay of 1 s (=1000000µS) to keep PA0 in this state. Then the loop repeats.

Faster code for the same application that uses the inline assembler is shown in **Listing 50**.

Listing 50.

```
from pyb import Pin, Timer
p_comp = Pin('A0')
tim5 = Timer(5, prescaler=83, period=0x3fffffff)
ch1 = tim5.channel(1, Timer.OC_ACTIVE, compare=5000000, \
polarity=Timer.HIGH, pin=p_comp)
@micropython.asm_thumb
def set_pin():
    movwt(r0, stm.TIM5)
    ldr(r1, [r0, stm.TIM_CR1])
    movw(r2, 0xfffe)
    and_(r1, r2)
    str(r1, [r0, stm.TIM_CR1])
    movw(r1, 0b100<<4)
    str(r1, [r0, stm.TIM_CCMR1])
    lsr(r1, r1, 2)
    str(r1, [r0, stm.TIM_CCMR1])
    ldr(r1, [r0, stm.TIM_CNT])
    eor(r1, r1)
    str(r1, [r0, stm.TIM_CNT])
    ldr(r1, [r0, stm.TIM_CR1])
    movw(r2, 1)
    orr(r1, r2)
    str(r1, [r0, stm.TIM_CR1])
while True:
    set_pin()
    while tim5.counter() < 6000000: continue
```

One more timer mode that may be useful for driving output pins is OC_TOGGLE. When a timer operates in this mode, the compare output pin will be toggled each time a compare match occurs. In the following example (**Listing 51**) pin PA0 is toggled every 10 s.

Listing 51.

```
from pyb import Pin, Timer
p_comp = Pin('A0')
tim5 = Timer(5, prescaler=83, period=0x3fffffff)
ch1 = tim5.channel(1, Timer.OC_TOGGLE, compare=10000000,\
polarity=Timer.HIGH, pin=p_comp)
while True:
    if tim5.counter() > 10000000:
        tim5.counter(0)
```

In this code, after pin PA0 is toggled, the code within **while True** loop clears the counter of Timer 5 (object **tim5**) by the statement

```
if tim5.counter() > 10000000:
    tim5.counter(0)
```

This forces the counter to start incrementing its value from 0 instead of running to the maximum value that is defined by the **period** parameter (=0x3fffffff).
We can further optimize the code in **Listing 51** by setting parameters **period** and **compare** to the same value (**Listing 52**). In this case, the counter will be reloaded with 0 simultaneously with toggling pin PA0.

Listing 52.

```
from pyb import Pin, Timer
p_comp = Pin('A0')
tim5 = Timer(5, prescaler=83, period=10000001)
ch1 = tim5.channel(1, Timer.OC_TOGGLE, compare=10000000,\
polarity=Timer.HIGH, pin=p_comp)
```

With this code, pin PA0 is toggled every 10 s. To set other interval, simply assign the new value to both **period** and **compare** parameters.

Measuring the pulse width of signals

Pulse width measurement is one of the most common tasks implemented by embedded code. There are various ways to measure the pulse width of a signal arriving on some digital input. One common method for measuring a pulse width is to calculate the number of counter ticks passing between the rising and falling edges of a pulse (**Fig.22**).

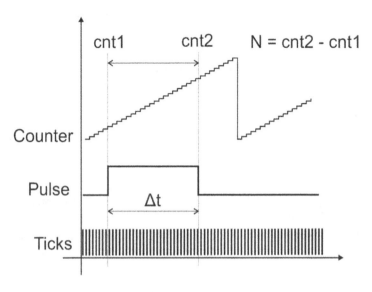

$$\Delta t = t_{period} \times N$$

N - number of ticks

t_{period} - period of ticks

Δt - pulse width

Fig.22

A simple example code (**Listing 53**) illustrates how to measure the width of a positive pulse on pin PC6 ('Y2') of PYBv1.1.

Listing 53.

```
from pyb import Pin, Timer
import time
p_in = Pin('Y2', Pin.IN, Pin.PULL_UP)
```

```
tim2 = Timer(2, prescaler=83, period=0x3fffffff)
cnt = 0
while True:
    while (machine.mem32[stm.GPIOC + stm.GPIO_IDR] \
    & 0x40) != 0:
        continue
    while (machine.mem32[stm.GPIOC + stm.GPIO_IDR] \
    & 0x40) == 0:
        continue
    machine.mem32[stm.TIM2 + stm.TIM_CNT] = 0
    while (machine.mem32[stm.GPIOC + stm.GPIO_IDR] \
    & 0x40) != 0:
        continue
    cnt = machine.mem32[stm.TIM2 + stm.TIM_CNT]
    print(cnt)
    time.sleep(5)
```

In this code, pin 'Y2' is configured as the digital input with a pull-up resistor (option PULL_UP).

Timer 2 provides timestamps for rising and falling edges of a pulse. We select the period between the ticks of a counter equal to 1 μS. For the PYBv1.1 board, the clock feeding the counter of Timer 2 provides the frequency F = 84 MHz, therefore we assign the value 83 to Prescaler in order to get the interval of 1μS between ticks.

This is reflected by the following formulas:

f_{ticks} = 84MHz/(Prescaler + 1) = 84MHz/(83+1) = 1MHz

t_{ticks} = 1 / f_{ticks} = 10^{-6} s = 1μS = 1 microsecond

In the above formulas, f_{ticks} is a frequency of pulses (ticks) to the counter of Timer2, t_{ticks} is a period of ticks.

To calculate the interval T between two successive edges (a pulse width), we can multiply the number N of ticks passed between edges by the period t_{ticks}:

$$T = N \times t_{ticks}$$

In our example, interval t will be calculated in μS.

The above code repeats measurements within the **while True** loop every 5 s.

The **cnt** variable keeps the number of ticks passed during a positive level of a pulse. We need to start counting exactly when the rising (positive) edge of a pulse arrives, therefore the program waits until the next positive edge arrives on pin 'Y2'. This is performed by the following sequence:

```
while (machine.mem32[stm.GPIOC + stm.GPIO_IDR] & 0x40) != 0:
    continue
while (machine.mem32[stm.GPIOC + stm.GPIO_IDR] & 0x40) == 0:
    continue
```

Immediately after input 'Y2' is brought high, the following instruction clears the counter of Timer2 (TIM_CCNT):

```
machine.mem32[stm.TIM2 + stm.TIM_CNT] = 0
```

Then the code waits until the falling (negative) edge arrives by executing the **while()** statement:

```
while (machine.mem32[stm.GPIOC + stm.GPIO_IDR] & 0x40) != 0:
    continue
```

When this happens, the value of the counter is moved to variable **cnt**:

```
cnt = machine.mem32[stm.TIM2 + stm.TIM_CNT]
```

The value of **cnt** is then displayed by the **print(cnt)** function on the screen. The above code was tested using rectangular pulse trains fed to input 'Y2' of PYBv1.1. The measurements were provided at frequencies from 100 Hz to 20.0 KHz and a duty cycle between 20-60%. The precision of the measurements was about 5-7 μS that is quite enough for the applications measuring relatively long intervals of tens to hundreds of microseconds.

The faster code of the same application written in the MicroPython inline assembler is shown in **Listing 54**.

Listing 54.

```
from pyb import Pin, Timer
import time
p_in = Pin('Y1', Pin.IN, Pin.PULL_UP)
```

```
tim2 = Timer(2, prescaler=83, period=0x3fffffff)
cnt = 0
@micropython.asm_thumb
def clear_cnt():
    movwt(r0, stm.TIM2)
    movwt(r1, 0)
    str(r1, [r0, stm.TIM_CNT])
@micropython.asm_thumb
def get_cnt():
    movwt(r1, stm.TIM2)
    ldr(r0, [r1, stm.TIM_CNT])
@micropython.asm_thumb
def wait_1():
    movwt(r0, stm.GPIOC)
    label(next)
    ldr(r1, [r0, stm.GPIO_IDR])
    movwt(r2, 0x40)
    and_(r1, r2)
    cmp(r1, 0)
    bgt(exit)
    b(next)
    label(exit)
@micropython.asm_thumb
def wait_0():
    movwt(r0, stm.GPIOC)
    label(next)
    ldr(r1, [r0, stm.GPIO_IDR])
    movwt(r2, 0x40)
    and_(r1, r2)
    cmp(r1, 0)
    beq(exit)
    b(next)
    label(exit)

while True:
    wait_0()
    wait_1()
    clear_cnt()
    wait_0()
    cnt = get_cnt()
```

```
print(cnt)
time.sleep(5)
```

We can reach much higher precision of pulse width measurement with STM32F4xx MCU, if timers will operate in Input Capture mode.
In this mode, the Capture/Compare Register(s) (TIMx_CCRx) of a timer are used to latch the value of the counter after a transition detected by the corresponding ICx signal.
The simplified diagram (**Fig.23**) represents the basic concepts.

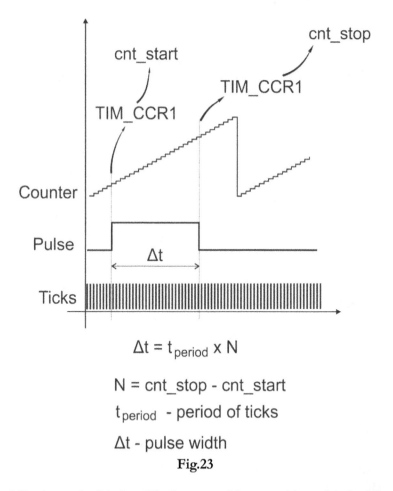

$$\Delta t = t_{period} \times N$$

$$N = cnt\_stop - cnt\_start$$

$$t_{period} - \text{period of ticks}$$

$$\Delta t - \text{pulse width}$$

Fig.23

The following code (**Listing 55**) allows to achieve precision of $1\mu S$ while performing measurements in a very wide range.

Listing 55.

```
from pyb import Pin, Timer
p = Pin('X6')
tim2 = Timer(2, prescaler=83, period=0x3fffffff)
ch1_cap = tim2.channel(1, Timer.IC, polarity=Timer.BOTH, pin=p)
import time
while True:
    while p.value() == 1: continue
    while p.value() == 0: continue
    cnt_start = machine.mem32[stm.TIM2 + stm.TIM_CCR1]
    while p.value() == 1: continue
    cnt_stop = machine.mem32[stm.TIM2 + stm.TIM_CCR1]
    delta = cnt_stop - cnt_start
    print(delta)
    time.sleep(8)
    tim2.counter(0)
```

This code was tested when a pulse train from a high-precision oscillator was fed to input PA5 ('X6') of PYBv1.1 board. There were no errors at the pulse train frequency as high as 25KHz (period = 40μS) and the pulse width as low as 20μS. The application provided no errors at the duty cycle from 30% to 51% at the frequency of 25KHz and duty cycle from 1% to 98% at the input frequency of 500 Hz.

To write more compact code than that from **Listing 55**, we replace high-level statements at the beginning of code with low-level functions from the **machine** module. This example (**Listing 56**) also helps to better understand how to configure Input Capture mode through the registers of Timer 2.

Listing 56.

```
from pyb import Pin
import time
p = Pin('X6', Pin.AF_PP, af=1)
machine.mem32[stm.RCC + stm.RCC_APB1ENR] |= 0b1
machine.mem32[stm.TIM2 + stm.TIM_PSC] = 83
machine.mem32[stm.TIM2 + stm.TIM_ARR] = 0x3fffffff
machine.mem32[stm.TIM2 + stm.TIM_CCER] &= 0xfffe
```

```
machine.mem32[stm.TIM2 + stm.TIM_CCMR1] |= 0b1
machine.mem32[stm.TIM2 + stm.TIM_CCER] |= 0b1011
machine.mem32[stm.TIM2 + stm.TIM_CR1] |= 0b1
while True:
    while p.value() == 0x1: continue
    while p.value() == 0x0: continue
    cnt_start = machine.mem32[stm.TIM2 + stm.TIM_CCR1]
    while p.value() == 0x1: continue
    cnt_stop = machine.mem32[stm.TIM2 + stm.TIM_CCR1]
    delta = cnt_stop - cnt_start
    print(delta)
    time.sleep(7)
    machine.mem32[stm.TIM2 + stm.TIM_CNT] = 0
```

In this code, we configure Channel 1 of Timer 2 using low-level instructions, therefore the size of code is reduced as compared with the previous example. Once Channel 1 of Timer 2 should operate in Input Capture mode, we select the suitable input pin and configure it to operate in alternate mode. In our case, we will use pin PA5. To assign this pin to the Channel 1 of Timer 2, we must know the index of an alternate function.
This information can be found in the datasheet on STM32F405/407 MCU (**Fig.24**).

Table 9. Alternate function mapping

Port		AF0 SYS	AF1 TIM1/2	AF2 TIM3/4/5	AF3 TIM8/9/10/11	AF4 I2C1/2/3	AF5 SPI1/SPI2/I2S2/I2S2ext
	PA0	-	TIM2_CH1_ETR	TIM 5_CH1	TIM8_ETR	-	-
	PA1	-	TIM2_CH2	TIM5_CH2	-	-	-
	PA2	-	TIM2_CH3	TIM5_CH3	TIM9_CH1	-	-
	PA3	-	TIM2_CH4	TIM5_CH4	TIM9_CH2	-	-
	PA4	-	-	-	-	-	SPI1_NSS
	PA5	-	TIM2_CH1_ETR	-	TIM8_CH1N	-	SPI1_SCK
	PA6	-	TIM1_BKIN	TIM3_CH1	TIM8_BKIN	-	SPI1_MISO

Fig.24

It is seen that pin PA5 should be assigned the alternate function AF1. To configure this pin, we use the statement

p = Pin('X6', Pin.AF_PP, af=1)

Then we start configuring Timer 2. The first what we should do is to enable clocking the timer by setting bit 1 in the RCC APB1 peripheral clock enable register (RCC_APB1ENR) shown in **Fig.25**.

7.3.13 RCC APB1 peripheral clock enable register (RCC_APB1ENR)

31	30	29	28	27	26	25	24	23	22	21	20	19	18	17	16
Reserved		DAC EN	PWR EN	Reserved	CAN2 EN	CAN1 EN	Reserved	I2C3 EN	I2C2 EN	I2C1 EN	UART5 EN	UART4 EN	USART3 EN	USART2 EN	Reserved
		rw	rw		rw	rw		rw	rw	rw	rw	rw	rw	rw	

15	14	13	12	11	10	9	8	7	6	5	4	3	2	1	0
SPI3 EN	SPI2 EN	Reserved		WWDG EN	Reserved		TIM14 EN	TIM13 EN	TIM12 EN	TIM7 EN	TIM6 EN	TIM5 EN	TIM4 EN	TIM3 EN	TIM2 EN
rw	rw			rw			rw	rw	rw	rw	rw	rw	rw	rw	rw

Fig.25

To set bit 1, the following instruction will be executed:

machine.mem32[stm.RCC + stm.RCC_APB1ENR] |= 0b1

At the next step, we configuring the counter of Timer 2 by the sequence:

machine.mem32[stm.TIM2 + stm.TIM_PSC] = 83
machine.mem32[stm.TIM2 + stm.TIM_ARR] = 0x3fffffff

With the frequency = 84 MHz provided to Timer 2 by the clock source, the value 83 in the TIM_PSC register provides the period between ticks = 1 µS. The value written into register TIM_ARR is selected to be very big to provide long time counting without overflow.

Once done, we begin to configure Channel 1 of Timer 2. In order to access configuration bit(s) in the capture/compare mode register 1 (TIMx_CCMR1), we need to disable Channel 1 first. This can be done by writing 0 into bit CC1E (**Fig.26**) in the capture/compare enable register TIM_CCER.

18.4.9   TIMx capture/compare enable register (TIMx_CCER)

15	14	13	12	11	10	9	8	7	6	5	4	3	2	1	0
CC4NP	Res.	CC4P	CC4E	CC3NP	Res.	CC3P	CC3E	CC2NP	Res.	CC2P	CC2E	CC1NP	Res.	CC1P	CC1E
rw		rw	rw	rw		rw	rw	rw		rw	rw	rw		rw	rw

Fig.26

The following statement clears bit CC1E:

machine.mem32[stm.TIM2 + stm.TIM_CCER] &= 0xfffe

Then we are capable to configure Channel 1 as input by the statement

machine.mem32[stm.TIM2 + stm.TIM_CCMR1] |= 0b1

This statement writes the value 0b01 into the CC1S[1:0] bits of the capture/compare mode register 1 (TIMx_CCMR1) as is shown in **Fig.27**.

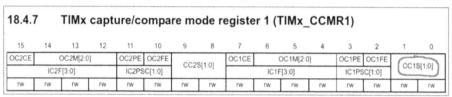

Fig.27

The last step in the configuration sequence for Channel 1 is to assign specific values for bits CC1NP and CC1P in register TIM_CCER and set bit CC1E as is shown in **Fig.28**. Bits CC1NP and CC1P define the polarity for trigger or capture operations. In our case, the input circuit should be sensitive to both TIxFP1 rising and falling edges, therefore we assign combination 0b11 to these bits.

18.4.9   TIMx capture/compare enable register (TIMx_CCER)

15	14	13	12	11	10	9	8	7	6	5	4	3	2	1	0
CC4NP	Res.	CC4P	CC4E	CC3NP	Res.	CC3P	CC3E	CC2NP	Res.	CC2P	CC2E	CC1NP	Res.	CC1P	CC1E
rw		rw	rw	rw		rw	rw	rw		rw	rw	rw		rw	rw

Fig.28

These bits are configured by the statement

machine.mem32[stm.TIM2 + stm.TIM_CCER] |= 0b1011

This statement ends configuration procedure for Channel 1 of Timer 2. The last statement enables Timer 2 by setting bit CEN in the control register 1 (TIMx_CR1):

machine.mem32[stm.TIM2 + stm.TIM_CR1] |= 0b1

The last example (**Listing 57**) is the optimized version of the code from **Listing 56**. In this code, we use the functions written in an inline assembler to improve the performance when measuring a pulse width. As in the previous example, we use Channel 1 of Timer 2 configured to operate in Input Capture (IC) mode. The pulse train to be measured arrives on pin PA5 ('X6') of the PYBv1.1 board.

Listing 57.

```
from pyb import Pin
import time
import array
ticks = array.array('i', [0, 0, 0])
p = Pin('X6', Pin.AF_PP, af=1)
machine.mem32[stm.RCC + stm.RCC_APB1ENR] |= 0b1
machine.mem32[stm.TIM2 + stm.TIM_PSC] = 83
machine.mem32[stm.TIM2 + stm.TIM_ARR] = 0x3fffffff
machine.mem32[stm.TIM2 + stm.TIM_CCER] &= 0xfffe
machine.mem32[stm.TIM2 + stm.TIM_CCMR1] |= 0b1
machine.mem32[stm.TIM2 + stm.TIM_CCER] |= 0b1011
machine.mem32[stm.TIM2 + stm.TIM_CR1] |= 0b1
@micropython.asm_thumb
def read_capture():
    movwt(r0, stm.TIM2)
    ldr(r0, [r0, stm.TIM_CCR1])
@micropython.asm_thumb
def clear_cnt():
    movwt(r0, stm.TIM2)
    movwt(r1, 0)
    str(r1, [r0, stm.TIM_CNT])
while True:
    while p.value() == 1: continue
    while p.value() == 0: continue
    ticks[0] = read_capture()
    while p.value() == 1: continue
    ticks[1] = read_capture()
    ticks[2] = ticks[1] - ticks[0]
    print(ticks[2])
    clear_cnt()
    time.sleep(7)
```

Configuring Channel 1 of Timer 2 for Input Capture mode is exactly the same as in the previous example, therefore we will skip the description of configuration steps for the timer.

In this code, we define two functions, **read_capture()** and **clear_cnt()**. The **read_capture()** function performs fast reading the contents of the capture/compare register 1 (TIMx_CCR1). The **clear_cnt()** function provides fast clearing the counter of Timer 2 – this is needed to avoid overflowing of Timer 2 when the application is running long time.

The value of a pulse width is calculated as the difference between the end ticks value (**ticks[1]**) and start ticks value (**ticks[0]**). The pulse width value is stored in the element **ticks[2]** of the **ticks** array after capturing the start and end values by the **read_capture()** function:

ticks[2] = ticks[1] - ticks[0]

Measurements of a pulse width are performed every 7 s. Each iteration begins with the sequence

while p.value() == 1: continue
while p.value() == 0: continue

that determines the start point ("0-1" transition of an input signal) for capturing.
This code provides very high precision measurements (error = 1 µS max) of rectangular pulse trains with a frequency up to 30 KHz (Period=33µS) and a pulse width as low as 14 µS.

Measuring the period of pulse trains

Once we know how to measure a pulse width, we can easily measure the period of a pulse train. The common approach to measure a period is illustrated in **Fig.29**.

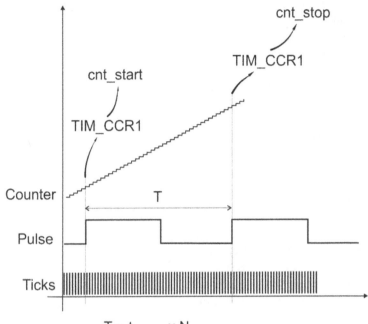

$$T = t_{period} \times N$$

$$N = cnt\_stop - cnt\_start$$

t_{period} - period of ticks

T - period of a pulse train

Fig.29

With this approach, when a rising edge arrives on a Capture Input pin of a timer, the value of a counter automatically goes into register TIM_CCR1. The program code should save the contents of TIM_CCR1 in some variable, say, **cnt_start**. When a next rising edge arrives, the updated value of a counter stored in register TIM_CCR1 goes to variable **cnt_stop**. The difference N between **cnt_stop** and **cnt_start** is then multiplied by the period of ticks, giving us the period of a pulse train.
The following source code (**Listing 58**) illustrates this approach.

Listing 58.

```
from pyb import Pin, Timer
tim2 = Timer(2, prescaler=83, period=0x3fffffff)
```

```
ch1 = tim2.channel(1, Timer.IC, polarity=Timer.BOTH, pin=Pin('A5'))
import time
@micropython.asm_thumb
def get_cap_reg():
    movwt(r0, stm.TIM2)
    ldr(r0, [r0, stm.TIM_CCR1])
@micropython.asm_thumb
def read_pin():
    movwt(r0, stm.GPIOA)
    ldr(r0, [r0, stm.GPIO_IDR])
    movw(r1, 1<<5)
    and_(r0, r1)
    lsr(r0, r0, 5)
while True:
    while read_pin() == 1: continue
    while read_pin() == 0: continue
    cnt_start = get_cap_reg()
    while read_pin() == 1: continue
    while read_pin() == 0: continue
    cnt_stop = get_cap_reg()
    delta = cnt_stop - cnt_start
    print(delta)
    time.sleep(10)
    tim2.counter(0)
```

This code allows to measure the period (frequency) of signals with high precision. The minimal error (=1 µS) was produced for the signals with a period = 20 µS (frequency = 50 KHz) and a duty cycle of 70%. The maximum error (= 28 µS) was exhibited for the signals with a period of 1.901s (=1901000 µS = 1901mS) that corresponds the frequency of about 0.53Hz. In that case, the measured value was as high as 1900972 µS = 1900.72mS.

One more approach to measure the frequency is to use Real-Time Clock (RTC). The following code (**Listing 59**) allows to perform the high-precision measurements of frequencies from 10 Hz to 33 KHz.

Listing 59.

from pyb import Pin, RTC

```
import time
pa15 = Pin('A15', Pin.OUT_PP)
callback = lambda r: pyb.Pin('A15').high()
p_in = Pin('Y1', Pin.IN, Pin.PULL_NONE)
pulses = 0
rtc1 = RTC()
rtc1.wakeup(1000, callback)
while True:
    pulses = 0
    pa15.low()
    rtc1.wakeup(1000, callback)
    while pa15.value() == 0:
    while p_in.value() == 1: continue
    while p_in.value() == 0: continue
    pulses += 1
    print(pulses)
    time.sleep(5)
```

In this code, variable **rtc1** is configured to wake-up after 1 s (1000 mS) expires. The callback function simply drives the orange LED (pin A15) ON after 1 s.

The input pulse train arrives on pin 'Y1'. In order to count a single pulse, the code detects the transition '1-0' by the sequence

```
while p_in.value() == 1: continue
while p_in.value() == 0: continue
```

When such transition occurs, the counter of pulses (variable **pulses**) is incremented by 1. The pulses are being counted until the output pin PA15 (variable **pa15**) is kept low. This is checked by the statement.

```
while pa15.value() == 0
```

After 1 s interval expires, RTC wakes-up, the output PA15 goes high and counting is stopped. The value kept in variable **pulses** gives the number of pulses detected on the input **p_in** (pin 'Y1' of PYBv1.1). This value will be equal to the frequency of an input signal in Hz.

One more useful application where Input Capture mode comes in handy is to detect short pulses. The common method to implement this task is illustrated in **Fig.30**.

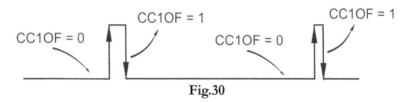

Fig.30

The MicroPython example code that allows to detect pulses on pin PA5 ('X6') of PYBv1.1 is shown in **Listing 60**.

Listing 60.

```
from pyb import Pin
p = Pin('X6', Pin.AF_PP, af=1)
machine.mem32[stm.RCC + stm.RCC_APB1ENR] |= 0b1
machine.mem32[stm.TIM2 + stm.TIM_PSC] = 83
machine.mem32[stm.TIM2 + stm.TIM_ARR] = 0x3ffffff
machine.mem32[stm.TIM2 + stm.TIM_CCER] &= 0xfffe
machine.mem32[stm.TIM2 + stm.TIM_CCMR1] |= 0b1
machine.mem32[stm.TIM2 + stm.TIM_CCER] |= 0b1011
machine.mem32[stm.TIM2 + stm.TIM_CR1] |= 0b1
cnt = 0
while True:
    while p.value() == 1: continue
    while p.value() == 0: continue
    machine.mem32[stm.TIM2 + stm.TIM_SR] &= 0xfdfd
    while machine.mem32[stm.TIM2 + stm.TIM_SR] and 0x200 == 0:
        continue
    cnt += 1
print(cnt, " pulses detected.")
```

In this code, we configure Channel 1 of Timer 2 to operate in Input Capture mode. We also configure the input circuit to be sensitive to both edges of input signal arriving on pin PA5 ('X6').
To detect the pulse, we need to know when '0-1' (rising edge) and '1-0' (falling edge) transitions occur. To check these conditions, the code reads bit CC1OF in the status register TIM_SR:

94

```
while machine.mem32[stm.TIM2 + stm.TIM_SR] and 0x200 == 0:
    continue
```

Note that bit CC1OF could already be set by the previous pulse, therefore the CC1OF and CC1IF bits should be previously cleared by the statement

```
machine.mem32[stm.TIM2 + stm.TIM_SR] &= 0xfdfd
```

After a pulse has been detected, the counter of pulses (variable **cnt**) is incremented and the value of **cnt** is displayed on the screen.
This code was tested by a sequence of short pulses (pulse width = 20µS) going with interval of 5 s.

Programming PWM

This section discusses in detail operating timers in PWM mode. The MicroPython Timer module provides various options to control PWM. The numerous code snippets described in MicroPython Documentation can also help you in programming PWM.
In this section, we discuss how to gain much more control over PWM using low-level programming techniques.
The very first demo example (**Listing 61**) illustrates how to write compact code for PYBv1.1 that allows to generate PWM signal with a base frequency of 1000 Hz (1.0KHz) on the compare output of Channel 1 of Timer 5.

Listing 61.

```
from pyb import Pin
p = Pin('A0', Pin.AF_PP, af=2)
machine.mem32[stm.RCC + stm.RCC_APB1ENR] |= 1<<3
machine.mem32[stm.TIM5 + stm.TIM_PSC] = 83
machine.mem32[stm.TIM5 + stm.TIM_ARR] = 999
machine.mem32[stm.TIM5 + stm.TIM_CCMR1] |= 0b111<<4
machine.mem32[stm.TIM5 + stm.TIM_CCER] |= 0b1
machine.mem32[stm.TIM5 + stm.TIM_CCR1] = 400
machine.mem32[stm.TIM5 + stm.TIM_CR1] |= 0b1
```

Despite its simplicity, the above code requires understanding a few basic principles of programming PWM.

To provide the PWM signal on some output, we should first know what pin can be used for this task. Each Timer channel may be assigned one of several predetermined pins. To do this, we should consult the datasheet on STM32F405/407 MCU where we need to examine alternate function mapping.

The fragment of interest is shown in **Fig.31**. The prime candidate to operate as the compare output for Channel 1 of Timer 5 is pin PA0 that is associated with alternate function AF2.

Table 9. Alternate function mapping

Port	AF0	AF1	AF2	AF3	AF4
	SYS	TIM1/2	TIM3/4/5	TIM8/9/10/11	I2C1/2/3
PA0	.	TIM2_CH1_ETR	TIM 5_CH1	TIM8_ETR	.
PA1	.	TIM2_CH2	TIM5_CH2	.	.
PA2	.	TIM2_CH3	TIM5_CH3	TIM9_CH1	.
PA3	.	TIM2_CH4	TIM5_CH4	TIM9_CH2	.
PA4	.	.	.	.	.

Fig.31

Therefore, what should we do first is to configure pin PA0 for alternate function by the statement:

p = Pin('A0', Pin.AF_PP, af=2)

That is all what we do with this pin. **Note** that you can select any other pin that is associated with Channel 1 of Timer 5.

Once we decided to configure PWM manually, we should take a care of all details.

96

Each timer operates only if its counter is fed by some clock source. Clock sources are disconnected from timers by default, therefore we should manually enable clocking to Timer 5. That is done by the statement

machine.mem32[stm.RCC + stm.RCC_APB1ENR] |= 1<<3

This statement sets bit 3 responsible for clocking Timer 5 in the RCC APB1 peripheral clock enable register (RCC_APB1ENR) (**Fig.32**).

7.3.13 RCC APB1 peripheral clock enable register (RCC_APB1ENR)

31	30	29	28	27	26	25	24	23	22	21	20	19	18	17	16
Reserved		DAC EN	PWR EN	Reserved	CAN2 EN	CAN1 EN	Reserved	I2C3 EN	I2C2 EN	I2C1 EN	UART5 EN	UART4 EN	USART3 EN	USART2 EN	Reserved
		rw	rw		rw	rw		rw	rw	rw	rw	rw	rw	rw	
15	14	13	12	11	10	9	8	7	6	5	4	3	2	1	0
SPI3 EN	SPI2 EN	Reserved		WWDG EN	Reserved		TIM14 EN	TIM13 EN	TIM12 EN	TIM7 EN	TIM6 EN	TIM5 EN	TIM4 EN	TIM3 EN	TIM2 EN
rw	rw			rw			rw	rw	rw	rw	rw	rw	rw	rw	rw

Fig.32

Since we decided to use the base PWM frequency of 1000 Hz, we need to configure both Prescaler and Period of the timer by writing correct values into registers TIM_PSC and TIM_ARR, respectively:

machine.mem32[stm.TIM5 + stm.TIM_PSC] = 83
machine.mem32[stm.TIM5 + stm.TIM_ARR] = 999

The clock feeding the counter of Timer 5 provides the frequency of 84 MHz, therefore the frequency on the compare output of Channel 1 will be as high as

$84\text{MHz}/(\text{prescaler}+1)/(\text{period}+1) = 84\text{MHz}/(83+1)/(999+1) = 1000 \text{ Hz}$

Now we can start configuring the compare output of Channel 1. First, set the mode of the output through the capture/compare register 1 (TIM_CCMR1) shown in **Fig.33**.

97

15	14	13	12	11	10	9	8	7	6	5	4	3	2	1	0
OC2CE	OC2M[2:0]			OC2PE	OC2FE	CC2S[1:0]		OC1CE	OC1M[2:0]			OC1PE	OC1FE	CC1S[1:0]	
	IC2F[3:0]			IC2PSC[1:0]					IC1F[3:0]			IC1PSC[1:0]			
rw	rw	rw	rw	rw	rw	rw	rw	rw	rw	rw	rw	rw	rw	rw	rw

Fig.33

In this register, bits 6:4 named OC1M(2:0) define compare mode of the Channel 1 output. In our case, we select mode PWM 2 that corresponds to combination 0b111 of these bits. This combination is written into bits OC1M(2:0) by the statement

machine.mem32[stm.TIM5 + stm.TIM_CCMR1] |= 0b111<<4

At the next step, we should configure the compare output itself. To do this, we should access the capture/compare enable register TIM_CCER. Usually, two options are needed to configure the output. First, we must enable the output pin (PA0, in our case) associated with the compare output of Channel 1 by setting bit CC1E. Second, we may set the polarity of active state (low or high, bit CC1P for Channel 1). These bits are shown in **Fig.34**.

18.4.9   TIMx capture/compare enable register (TIMx_CCER)

15	14	13	12	11	10	9	8	7	6	5	4	3	2	1	0
CC4NP	Res.	CC4P	CC4E	CC3NP	Res.	CC3P	CC3E	CC2NP	Res.	CC2P	CC2E	CC1NP	Res.	CC1P	CC1E
rw		rw	rw	rw		rw	rw	rw		rw	rw	rw		rw	rw

Fig.34

What we need in our case is to enable the output pin (bit CC1E) by the statement

machine.mem32[stm.TIM5 + stm.TIM_CCER] |= 0b1

If bit CC1P is clear (by default), the pulse width of the output signal is determined as the difference between the contents of TIM_ARR+1 and TIM_CCR1. In our case, the pulse width will be equal to

$$TIM\_ARR - TIM\_CCR1 + 1 = 999 - 400 + 1 = 600$$

Therefore, the duty cycle of a PWM signal will be equal to 600/1000 x 100 = 60%. If we set bit CC1P in register TIM_CCR1, then the value in register TIM_CCR1 will directly define the pulse width. Therefore, if we replace the statement

machine.mem32[stm.TIM5 + stm.TIM_CCER] |= 0b1

with

machine.mem32[stm.TIM5 + stm.TIM_CCER] |= 0b11

than the value written in the TIM_CCR1 register (600, in our case) will directly define the pulse width and consequently a duty cycle.

The last statement in the sequence starts Timer 5 by enabling its counter:

machine.mem32[stm.TIM5 + stm.TIM_CR1] |= 0b1

The next two examples are developed for STM32F4DISCOVERY. The codes in **Listing 62 – Listing 63** illustrate configuring PWM for Channel 1 (pin PB6) and Channel 2 (pin PB7) of Timer 4, respectively.

Listing 62.

```
machine.mem32[stm.GPIOB + stm.GPIO_MODER] |= 0b10<<12
machine.mem32[stm.GPIOB + 0x20] |= 0b10<<24
machine.mem32[stm.RCC + stm.RCC_APB1ENR] |= 1<<2
machine.mem32[stm.TIM4 + stm.TIM_ARR] = 999
machine.mem32[stm.TIM4 + stm.TIM_PSC] = 83
machine.mem32[stm.TIM4 + stm.TIM_CCMR1] |= 0b111<<4
machine.mem32[stm.TIM4 + stm.TIM_CCER] |= 0b1
machine.mem32[stm.TIM4 + stm.TIM_CCR1] = 230
machine.mem32[stm.TIM4 + stm.TIM_CR1] |= 0b1
```

Listing 63.

```
machine.mem32[stm.GPIOB + stm.GPIO_MODER] |= 0b10<<14
machine.mem32[stm.GPIOB + 0x20] |= 0b10<<28
machine.mem32[stm.RCC + stm.RCC_APB1ENR] |= 1<<2
```

```
machine.mem32[stm.TIM4 + stm.TIM_ARR] = 99
machine.mem32[stm.TIM4 + stm.TIM_PSC] = 83
machine.mem32[stm.TIM4 + stm.TIM_CCMR1] |= 0b111<<12
machine.mem32[stm.TIM4 + stm.TIM_CCER] |= 0b1<<4
machine.mem32[stm.TIM4 + stm.TIM_CCR2] = 17
machine.mem32[stm.TIM4 + stm.TIM_CR1] |= 0b1
```

Note that output Channels 1-2 of timers are configured through the capture/compare mode register 1 (TIM_CCMR1), while channels 3-4 are configured through the capture/compare mode register 1 (TIM_CCMR2). Also, the compare value for each output channel should be written to the corresponding capture/compare register (TIM_CCRx, x=1...4).
The following example (**Listing 64**) illustrates configuring the PWM output of Channel 3 of Timer 2 of PYBv1.1 for operating in PWM mode.

Listing 64.

```
machine.mem32[stm.GPIOB + stm.GPIO_MODER] |= 0b10<<20
machine.mem32[stm.GPIOB + 0x24] |= 0b0001<<8
machine.mem32[stm.RCC + stm.RCC_APB1ENR] |= 0x1
machine.mem32[stm.TIM2 + stm.TIM_PSC] = 83
machine.mem32[stm.TIM2 + stm.TIM_ARR] = 999
machine.mem32[stm.TIM2 + stm.TIM_CCMR2] |= 0b111<<4
machine.mem32[stm.TIM2 + stm.TIM_CCER] |= 0b1<<8
machine.mem32[stm.TIM2 + stm.TIM_CCR3] = 370
machine.mem32[stm.TIM2 + stm.TIM_CR1] |= 0b1
```

The output of Channel 3 may be assigned pin PB10 ('Y9') of port GPIOB. The alternate function for this pin is AF1 (= 0b0001), therefore we configure this pin through registers GPIO_MODER and GPIO_AFRH by the sequence:

```
machine.mem32[stm.GPIOB + stm.GPIO_MODER] |= 0b10<<20
machine.mem32[stm.GPIOB + 0x24] |= 0b0001<<8
```

Then we enable clocking the counter of Timer 2:

```
machine.mem32[stm.RCC + stm.RCC_APB1ENR] |= 0x1
```

In this application, we want to gain the frequency of 1.0KHz on pin PB10 (period = 1 mS). The clock source feeding the counter of Timer 2 provides the frequency of 83 MHz, therefore registers TIM_PSC and TIM_ARR should be configured as follows:

```
machine.mem32[stm.TIM2 + stm.TIM_PSC] = 83
machine.mem32[stm.TIM2 + stm.TIM_ARR] = 999
```

To configure the compare mode (PWM 2) for Channel 3, we will use register TIM_CCMR2 in the statement:

```
machine.mem32[stm.TIM2 + stm.TIM_CCMR2] |= 0b111<<4
```

The next step is to enable the signal on the corresponding output pin through the capture/compare enable register TIM_CCER by the statement:

```
machine.mem32[stm.TIM2 + stm.TIM_CCER] |= 0b1<<8
```

To complete configuring Channel 3, we should write the desired compare value into the capture/compare register TIM_CCR3. Assume, we need the duty cycle of an output pulse train to be 63%. At the given configuration of Channel 3, we should write the value 370 in TIM_CCR3:

```
machine.mem32[stm.TIM2 + stm.TIM_CCR3] = 370
```

Finally, we start Timer 3 by the statement:

```
machine.mem32[stm.TIM2 + stm.TIM_CR1] |= 0b1
```

In the above configuration, the active state of the output is high (bit CC3P in register TIM_CCER is 0).
To change the active state of the output OC3 to low, we should write 1 in the compare polarity bit CC3P by the statement:

```
machine.mem32[stm.TIM2 + stm.TIM_CCER] |= 0b11<<8
```

To write faster code, we can use the MicroPython inline assembler. The following example (**Listing 65**) illustrates this approach for configuring PWM of Channel 3 of Timer 2. Here, the function **config_tim2_pwm()**

takes a single parameter that is a duty cycle calculated for the base frequency = 1000 Hz.

Listing 65.

```
@micropython.asm_thumb
def config_tim2_pwm(r0):
    movwt(r1, stm.TIM2)
    ldr(r2, [r1, stm.TIM_CR1])
    movw(r3, 1)
    bic(r2, r3)
    str(r2, [r1, stm.TIM_CR1])
    movwt(r1, stm.GPIOB)
    ldr(r2, [r1, stm.GPIO_MODER])
    movwt(r3, 0b10<<20)
    orr(r2, r3)
    str(r2, [r1, stm.GPIO_MODER])
    ldr(r2, [r1, 0x24])
    movwt(r3, 0b0001<<8)
    orr(r2, r3)
    str(r2, [r1, 0x24])
    movwt(r1, stm.RCC)
    ldr(r2, [r1, stm.RCC_APB1ENR])
    movw(r3, 0x1)
    orr(r2, r3)
    str(r2, [r1, stm.RCC_APB1ENR])
    movwt(r1, stm.TIM2)
    movw(r2, 83)
    str(r2, [r1, stm.TIM_PSC])
    movwt(r2, 999)
    str(r2, [r1, stm.TIM_ARR])
    movw(r3, 1)
    add(r2, r2, r3)
    movw(r3, 10)
    mul(r0, r3)
    sub(r2, r2, r0)
    str(r2, [r1, stm.TIM_CCR3])
    movwt(r3, 0b111<<4)
    ldr(r2, [r1, stm.TIM_CCMR2])
    orr(r2, r3)
```

```
str(r2, [r1, stm.TIM_CCMR2])
movwt(r3, 0b1<<8)
ldr(r2, [r1, stm.TIM_CCER])
orr(r2, r3)
str(r2, [r1, stm.TIM_CCER])
movw(r3, 1)
ldr(r2, [r1, stm.TIM_CR1])
orr(r2, r3)
str(r2, [r1, stm.TIM_CR1])
```

In this code, the sequence

```
movwt(r1, stm.TIM2)
ldr(r2, [r1, stm.TIM_CR1])
movw(r3, 1)
bic(r2, r3)
str(r2, [r1, stm.TIM_CR1])
```

stops the counter of Timer 2 by clearing bit CEN in the control register TIM_CR1.
Then the code assigns the alternate function to pin PB10 of port GPIOB through configuring corresponding bits in registers GPIO_MODER and GPIO_AFRH by the statements

```
movwt(r1, stm.GPIOB)
ldr(r2, [r1, stm.GPIO_MODER])
movwt(r3, 0b10<<20)
orr(r2, r3)
str(r2, [r1, stm.GPIO_MODER])
ldr(r2, [r1, 0x24])
movwt(r3, 0b0001<<8)
orr(r2, r3)
str(r2, [r1, 0x24])
```

At the next step, we enable clocking the counter of Timer 2 through setting bit 0 in register RCC_APB1ENR:

```
movwt(r1, stm.RCC)
ldr(r2, [r1, stm.RCC_APB1ENR])
movw(r3, 0x1)
```

```
orr(r2, r3)
str(r2, [r1, stm.RCC_APB1ENR])
```

The following code fragment writes the Prescaler and Period values into registers TIM_PSC and TIM_ARR, respectively.

```
movwt(r1, stm.TIM2)
movw(r2, 83)
str(r2, [r1, stm.TIM_PSC])
movwt(r2, 999)
str(r2, [r1, stm.TIM_ARR])
```

The parameter of the function **config_tim2_pwm()** is a duty cycle of a PWM signal. The parameter being passed in MCU register **r0** can range from 0 to 100, while the Period value (register TIM_ARR) is assigned 9999. For that reason, we should map the range of a duty cycle (0-100) into Period+1 (=1000). The mapped value should then be written in register TIM_CCR3. All these operations are implemented by the following sequence:

```
movw(r3, 1)
add(r2, r2, r3)
movw(r3, 10)
mul(r0, r3)
sub(r2, r2, r0)
str(r2, [r1, stm.TIM_CCR3])
```

To put Timer 2 in PWM 2 mode, we should write the value 0b111 in OC3M field (bits 4-6) of the capture/compare mode register TIM_CCMR2 by the sequence

```
movwt(r3, 0b111<<4)
ldr(r2, [r1, stm.TIM_CCMR2])
orr(r2, r3)
str(r2, [r1, stm.TIM_CCMR2])
```

The next step is to enable output signal on corresponding pin by setting bit CC3E in the capture/compare enable register TIM_CCER. This is done by the sequence

```
movwt(r3, 0b1<<8)
```

```
ldr(r2, [r1, stm.TIM_CCER])
orr(r2, r3)
str(r2, [r1, stm.TIM_CCER])
```

The last four assembler instructions start Timer 2 by enabling its counter:

```
movw(r3, 1)
ldr(r2, [r1, stm.TIM_CR1])
orr(r2, r3)
str(r2, [r1, stm.TIM_CR1])
```

Below are a couple of examples of how to set the duty cycle on Channel 3 through REPL:

```
>>> config_tim2_pwm(51)
510
>>> config_tim2_pwm(18)
180
>>> config_tim2_pwm(86)
860
```

Direct Digital Synthesis in MicroPython Applicatons

Due to availability of STM32F405/407 MCU that have on-chip digital-to-analog converters (DACs), both PYBv1.1 and STM32F4DISCOVERY boards are capable of producing sine, triangular and other wave form outputs.

The STM32 DAC module is a 12-bit, voltage output converter, with two output channels to support various audio applications such as analog waveform generation, security alarms, talking toys, answering machines, man-machine interfaces, low-cost music players, control engineering, etc.

The DAC can be configured in 8- or 12-bit mode. In 12-bit mode, the data could be left- or right-aligned. The DAC has two output channels, each with its own converter. In dual DAC channel mode, conversions could be done independently or simultaneously when both channels are grouped together for synchronous update operations.

To generate various waveforms, DAC uses a technique known as Direct Digital Synthesis (DDS). This involves the Digital-To-Analog Converter (DAC), Timer and Direct Memory Access (DMA) controller. DMA provides high-speed data transfer between peripherals and memory and between memory and memory. Data can be quickly moved by DMA without any CPU action, therefore the CPU resources are kept free for other operations. Specifically, the PYBv1.1 and STM32F4DISCOVERY boards can produce analog waveforms using DMA, Timer 6 (TIM6) and DAC peripherals as is illustrated in **Fig.35**.

DDS using STM32Fxx CPU

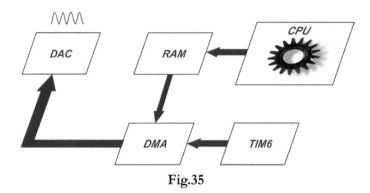

Fig.35

At start up, the code fills the buffer array located in RAM with data patterns for further reproducing some waveform, for example, sine wave. Then the data from the buffer array are transferred from RAM to DAC peripheral using DMA.
TIM6 is used to trigger the DAC that will convert the digital data to an analog waveform.

The basic example of implementing sine wave generation taken from MicroPython Documentation is shown below (**Listing 66**).

Listing 66.

```
from pyb import Pin, DAC
import math
dac1 = DAC(Pin('X5'))
buf = bytearray(100)
```

```
for i in range(len(buf)):
    buf[i] = 128 + int(127 * math.sin(2 * math.pi * i / len(buf)))
dac1.write_timed(buf, 400 * len(buf), mode=DAC.CIRCULAR)
```

Here, the **write_timed()** function initiates a burst of buffer array (variable **buf**) to the DAC Channel 1 (object **dac1**) using a DMA transfer. The input data is treated as an array of bytes in 8-bit mode. The elements of the **buf** array are writing with a frequency of 400 Hz using Timer 6. To generate continuous waveform, the DMA should circularly transfer data from RAM to DAC, therefore the mode is set to DAC.CIRCULAR.
By default, Timer 6 is used to trigger DAC samples, but we can also select Timer 2, 4, 5, 7 and 8.

The following example illustrates how to select Timer 7 instead of Timer 6 for triggering DAC samples of Channel 1. In order to understand how to select a trigger for Channel 1, let's look at **Fig.36** that shows the block diagram of a DAC channel.

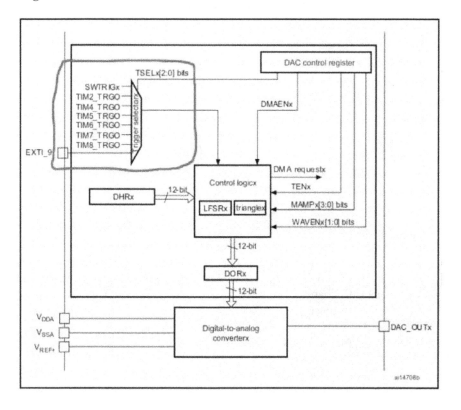

Fig.36

Selection of trigger is implemented using the Trigger selector. To select the desired trigger for a DAC channel, we should write the proper value into bits TSELx[2:0] of the DAC control register (DAC_CR) (**Fig.37**).

14.5.1			DAC control register (DAC_CR)											

31	30	29	28	27	26	25	24	23	22	21	20	19	18	17	16
Reserved		DMAU DRIE2	DMA EN2	MAMP2[3:0]				WAVE2[1:0]		TSEL2[2:0]			TEN2	BOFF2	EN2
		rw	rw	rw	rw	rw	rw	rw	rw	rw	rw	rw	rw	rw	rw
15	14	13	12	11	10	9	8	7	6	5	4	3	2	1	0
Reserved		DMAU DRIE1	DMA EN1	MAMP1[3:0]				WAVE1[1:0]		TSEL1[2:0]			TEN1	BOFF1	EN1
		rw	rw	rw	rw	rw	rw	rw	rw	rw	rw	rw	rw	rw	rw

Fig.37

Since we configure DAC Channel 1, we should operate with TSEL1[2:0] bits located in positions [5:3] in register DAC_CR. The possible values for the TSEL1[2:0] bits are shown in **Fig.38**.

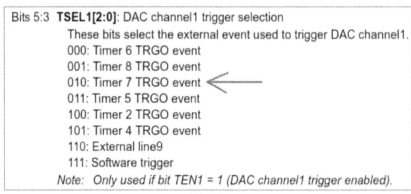

Bits 5:3 **TSEL1[2:0]**: DAC channel1 trigger selection
  These bits select the external event used to trigger DAC channel1.
  000: Timer 6 TRGO event
  001: Timer 8 TRGO event
  010: Timer 7 TRGO event
  011: Timer 5 TRGO event
  100: Timer 2 TRGO event
  101: Timer 4 TRGO event
  110: External line9
  111: Software trigger
  Note: Only used if bit TEN1 = 1 (DAC channel1 trigger enabled).

Fig.38

By default, bits TSEL1[2:0] are set to 0b000 thus selecting Timer 6 as a trigger for DAC Channel 1. Once we want to use Timer 7, we need to write a value 0b010 into these bits – that is shown by the red arrow. **Note** that bit TEN1 (bit 2 in DAC_CR) should be set – in our case, that is already done after invoking function **write_timed()**.

A few words about configuring frequency of a dedicated timer. As you can see from the above code, we select the output frequency on output pin PA4 ('X6') equal to 400 Hz. Once the size of the array **buf** is 100, the frequency of timer overflowing should be as high as 400 Hz x 100 = 40.0KHz. This corresponds to the period of 25 µS that more than enough to transfer the sample from RAM (array **buf**) to the 8-bit right aligned data holding register (DAC_DHR8R1) of DAC Channel 1.

It is clear that in order to get the higher output frequency on a DAC output pin, we need to decrease the period of a timer triggering DAC. If, for example, we need to get the DAC output frequency equal to 1000 Hz, we must increase the frequency of a timer up to 1000 x 100 = 100.0 KHz (period = 10 µS). The upper limit of the frequency of a timer depends on how much time is required to transfer data from RAM to DAC.

Let's go to practice and reconfigure the DAC Channel 1 of PYBv1.1 to be driven by Timer 7. We also want to set the output frequency of DAC Channel 1 to 500 Hz.
The configuration sequence for this case is shown below (**Listing 67**).

Listing 67.

```
from pyb import Timer
tim7 = Timer(7, freq=50000)
machine.mem32[stm.TIM7 + stm.TIM_CR2] &= ~(0b111 << 4)
machine.mem32[stm.TIM7 + stm.TIM_CR2] |= 0b010 << 4
machine.mem32[stm.DAC + stm.DAC_CR] &= ~0b1
machine.mem32[stm.DAC + stm.DAC_CR] &= ~(0b111 << 3)
machine.mem32[stm.DAC + stm.DAC_CR] |= 0b010 << 3
machine.mem32[stm.DAC + stm.DAC_CR] |= 0b1
```

In this sequence, the first 2 statements

```
from pyb import Timer
tim7 = Timer(7, freq=50000)
```

configure Timer 7. Since we need the DAC output frequency to be 500 Hz, the variable **tim7** should be configured to provide the frequency 500Hz x 100 = 50000 Hz = 50.0KHz.

Additionally, to initiate data transfer on DAC output each time the Timer 7 overflows, the trigger output (TRGO) should be provided for the DAC Channel 1. Therefore, we should assign the value 0b010 to bits MMS[2:0] in the TIM7 control register 2 (TIMx_CR2) by the following statements:

machine.mem32[stm.TIM7 + stm.TIM_CR2] &= ~(0b111 << 4)
machine.mem32[stm.TIM7 + stm.TIM_CR2] |= 0b010 << 4

That's all what we do with Timer 7. Then we should configure the DAC Channel 1. The configuration sequence begins with the statement

machine.mem32[stm.DAC + stm.DAC_CR] &= ~0b1

that disables DAC Channel 1.

Next we should configure bits TSEL1[2:0]. If these bits are already cleared, skip the next instruction, otherwise clear bits TSEL1[2:0] by the statement

machine.mem32[stm.DAC + stm.DAC_CR] &= ~(0b111 << 3)

Set the new trigger output (Timer 7 TRGO) for DAC Channel 1 by the statement

machine.mem32[stm.DAC + stm.DAC_CR] |= 0b010 << 3

Finally, start the DAC Channel 1 by the statement

machine.mem32[stm.DAC + stm.DAC_CR] |= 0b1

Now the DAC Channel is triggered by Timer 7 trigger output. We can change the output frequency of DAC Channel 1 by setting new frequency for Timer 7 as is shown below:

tim7.freq(60000)
tim7.freq(77000)
tim7.freq(98000)

The above 3 statements set the output frequency of DAC channel 1 to 600, 770 and 980Hz, respectively.

The DAC output can also be triggered by external signals that arrives on the EXTI_9 input that is nothing else as line 9 of external interrupt. This line may be assigned pin PA9, PB9, PC9, etc. In PYBv1.1, we can feed the external signal to pin PB9 ('Y4'). The hardware configuration for this example is shown in **Fig.39**.

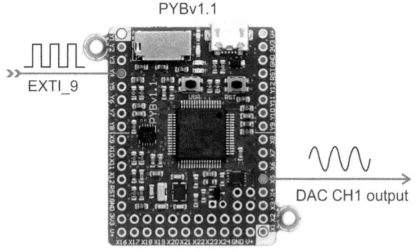

Fig.39

Again, since we configure DAC Channel 1, we should write the proper value in the TSEL1[2:0] bits located in positions [5:3] in register DAC_CR. For EXTI_9 trigger output, the combination of TSEL1[2:0] bits will be 0b110 (indicated by the arrow in **Fig.40**).

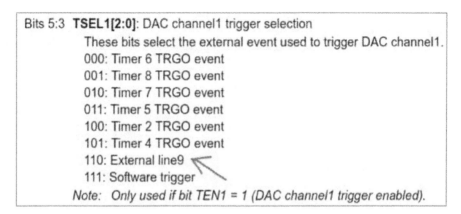

Bits 5:3 **TSEL1[2:0]**: DAC channel1 trigger selection
These bits select the external event used to trigger DAC channel1.
000: Timer 6 TRGO event
001: Timer 8 TRGO event
010: Timer 7 TRGO event
011: Timer 5 TRGO event
100: Timer 2 TRGO event
101: Timer 4 TRGO event
110: External line9
111: Software trigger
Note: Only used if bit TEN1 = 1 (DAC channel1 trigger enabled).

Fig.40

Configuring EXTI_9 as a trigger output involves a number of low-level instructions. We can significantly simplify this task by using the MicroPython class ExtInt for configuring external interrupts. In this case, the configurations sequence for PYBv1.1 involves the following steps.

First, configure the external interrupt on line 9 with input assigned to pin PB9 ('Y4').

```
from pyb import ExtInt
def callback(param):
    return
ext1 = ExtInt(Pin('Y4'), ExtInt.IRQ_RISING, \
Pin.PULL_NONE, callback)
```

Note that ISR code for the **ext1** interrupt (function **callback()**) does nothing – it immediately returns control to foreground (main) code.

Second, disable DAC Channel 1, write the value 0b110 into bits TSEL1[2:0] in the control register DAC_CR and enable DAC Channel 1. This is implemented by the following sequence:

```
machine.mem32[stm.DAC + stm.DAC_CR] &= ~0b1
machine.mem32[stm.DAC + stm.DAC_CR] &= ~(0b111 << 3)
machine.mem32[stm.DAC + stm.DAC_CR] |= 0b110 << 3
machine.mem32[stm.DAC + stm.DAC_CR] |= 0b1
```

Below is the same example but adapted for the STM32F4DISCOVERY board. Here we will also use the example code for generating sine wave with a frequency of 400 Hz as a template (**Listing 68**).

Listing 68.

```
from pyb import Pin, DAC
import math
dac1 = DAC(Pin('PA4'))
buf = bytearray(100)
for i in range(len(buf)):
    buf[i] = 128 + int(127 * math.sin(2 * math.pi * i / len(buf)))
```

```
dac1.write_timed(buf, 400 * len(buf), mode=DAC.CIRCULAR)
```

Let's configure the external interrupt on line 9 with input assigned to pin PC9 on the STM32F4DISCOVERY board.

```
from pyb import ExtInt
def callback(param):
    return
ext1 = ExtInt(Pin('PC9'), ExtInt.IRQ_RISING, \
Pin.PULL_NONE, callback)
```

Then configure the DAC Channel 1 by the sequence:

```
machine.mem32[stm.DAC + stm.DAC_CR] &= ~0b1
machine.mem32[stm.DAC + stm.DAC_CR] &= ~(0b111 << 3)
machine.mem32[stm.DAC + stm.DAC_CR] |= 0b110 << 3
machine.mem32[stm.DAC + stm.DAC_CR] |= 0b1
```

With DAC, it is easy to produce various wave forms as is illustrated in the following examples.
The sawtooth signal can be obtained using the source code from **Listing 69**.

Listing 69.

```
from pyb import DAC
import math
dac1 = DAC(1)
buf = bytearray(256)
for i in range(len(buf)):
    buf[i] = i
    i += 1
dac1.write_timed(buf, 1000 * len(buf), mode=DAC.CIRCULAR)
```

The frequency of this signal is set to 1000 Hz. The signal captured on pin PA4 of STM32F4DISCOVERY appears as follows (**Fig.41**).

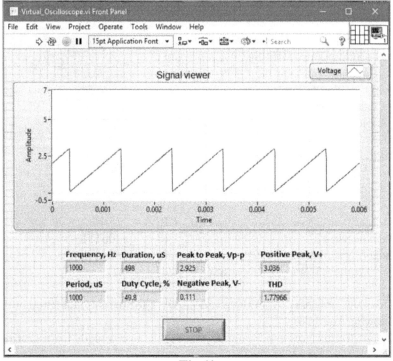

Fig.41

To change the slope of a sawtooth waveform, we can use the following code (**Listing 70**).

Listing 70.

```
from pyb import DAC
import math
dac1 = DAC(1)
buf = bytearray(256)
for i in range(len(buf)):
    buf[i] = len(buf) - i
    i += 1
dac1.write_timed(buf, 1000 * len(buf), mode=DAC.CIRCULAR)
```

Such a waveform captured on pin PA4 of STM32F4DISCOVERY is shown in **Fig.42**.

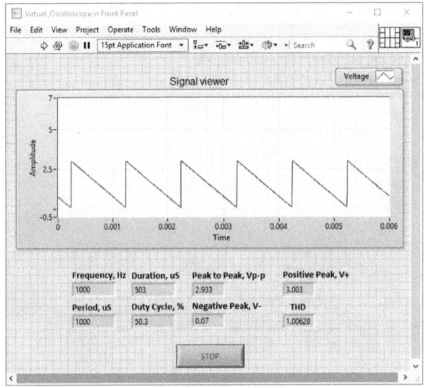

Fig.42

The following example (**Listing 71**) allows to obtain the trapezoid waveform on the DAC Channel 1 output.

Listing 71.

```
from pyb import DAC
import math
dac1 = DAC(1)
buf = bytearray(256)
for i in range(len(buf)):
    if i < 100: buf[i] = i
    else: buf[i] = 100
    i += 1
dac1.write_timed(buf, 1000 * len(buf), mode=DAC.CIRCULAR)
```

The trapezoid signal is shown **Fig.43**.

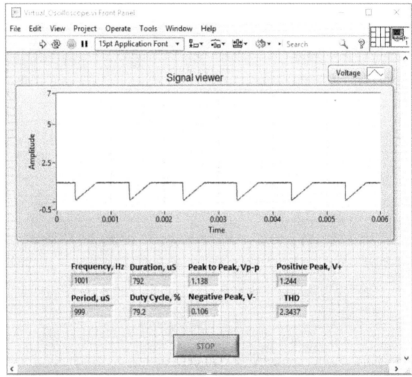

Fig.43

The triangle signal may be obtained using the following code (**Listing 72**).

Listing 72.

```
from pyb import DAC
import math
dac1 = DAC(1)
buf = bytearray(256)
for i in range(len(buf)):
    if i < len(buf)/2 : buf[i] = i
    else: buf[i] = len(buf) - i
    i += 1
```

The triangle signal on pin PA4 appears as follows (**Fig.44**).

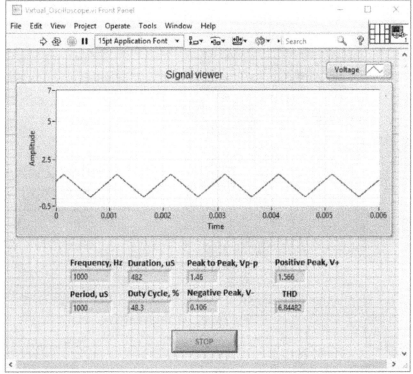

Fig.44

Analog-To-Digital Conversion in MicroPython applications

This section describes how to configure and control analog-to-digital conversion at low level. The code represented in this section can run on PYBv1.1 and other boards equipped with STM32F405/407 Cortex-M4 processors.
The basic circuit used in all examples is shown in **Fig.45**.

117

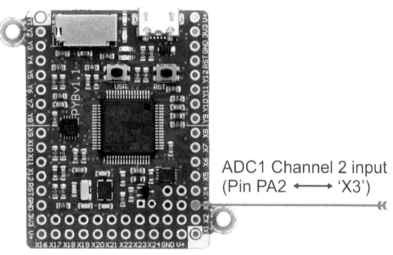

PYBv1.1

ADC1 Channel 2 input
(Pin PA2 ⟵⟶ 'X3')

Fig.45

In this circuit, the test analog signal is fed to Channel 2 of ADC1. The Channel 2 input is assigned pin PA2 of STM32F4xx MCU ('X3' on the PYBv1.1 board).

While discussing the example codes, we will refer to the following ADC registers as they appear in the STM32F405/407 Reference Manual:

- ADC control register 2 (ADC_CR2);
- ADC status register (ADC_SR);
- ADC regular data register (ADC_DR).

Let's consider the basics of A/D conversion on STM32F405/407 MCU. In Single conversion mode, the ADC performs only one conversion. This mode is started when the CONT bit in the ADC control register 2 (ADC_CR2) is clear (=0). To start a conversion, one of the following events should occur:

- the SWSTART bit in the ADC_CR2 register is set (for a regular channel only);
- the JSWSTART bit is set (for an injected channel);
- external trigger is active (for a regular or injected channel).

Once the conversion of the selected channel is complete (for a regular channel) then the following actions are executed:

- the converted data are stored into the 16-bit ADC_DR register;
- the EOC (end of conversion) flag is set;
- an interrupt is generated if the EOCIE bit is set.

If an injected channel was converted:
- the converted data are stored into the 16-bit ADC_JDR1 register;
- the JEOC (end of conversion injected) flag is set;
- an interrupt is generated if the JEOCIE bit is set.

Then the ADC stops and the next A/D conversion will start after bit SWSTART is set again.

The conversion process is illustrated by the timing diagram shown in **Fig.46**.

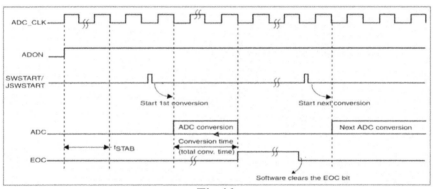

Fig.46

In this section, we will consider the conversion process only for a single regular ADC1 channel (Channel 2, in our case).

The following code (**Listing 73**) allows to perform periodical measurements on ADC1 Channel 2 input using Single conversion mode. To make the code fast, we use low-level statements from the **machine** module.

Listing 73.

```
from pyb import Pin
import time
a1_in2 = Pin('X3', Pin.ANALOG)
machine.mem32[stm.RCC + stm.RCC_APB2ENR] |= 1 << 8
machine.mem32[stm.ADC1 + stm.ADC_CR2] |= 0x1
machine.mem32[stm.ADC1 + stm.ADC_SQR1] &= ~(0xf << 20)
```

```
machine.mem32[stm.ADC1 + stm.ADC_SQR3] |= 0x2
Dn = 0
vin = 0.0
while True:
    machine.mem32[stm.ADC1 + stm.ADC_CR2] |= 0x1 << 30
    while (machine.mem32[stm.ADC1 + stm.ADC_SR] \
    & 0x2) == 0:
        continue
    Dn = machine.mem32[stm.ADC1 + stm.ADC_DR] & 0xfff
    vin = Dn * 3.33 / 4095
    print("ADC1 CH2 Input = %2.3f V" % vin)
    time.sleep(5)
```

In this and following code, we assume that the ADC registers are configured by default values (after power is on or reset).
The ADC1 Channel 2 should be assigned pin PA2 ('X3'), therefore we put this pin in analog mode by the statement

a1_in2 = Pin('X3', Pin.ANALOG)

Configuring ADC1 begins with enabling clock to the device through the RCC APB2 peripheral clock enable register (RCC_APB2ENR) by the statement

machine.mem32[stm.RCC + stm.RCC_APB2ENR] |= 1 << 8

When bit 8 (ADC1EN) of this register (**Fig.47**) is set, clocking ADC1 is enabled.

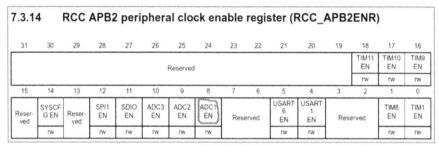

Fig.47

The rest of code operates with ADC registers. First, we enable ADC1 through the ADC control register 2 (ADC_CR2) shown in **Fig.48**.

13.13.3   ADC control register 2 (ADC_CR2)

31	30	29	28	27	26	25	24	23	22	21	20	19	18	17	16
reserved	SWSTART	EXTEN		EXTSEL[3:0]				reserved	JSWSTART	JEXTEN		JEXTSEL[3:0]			
	rw	rw	rw	rw	rw	rw	rw		rw	rw	rw	rw	rw	rw	rw

15	14	13	12	11	10	9	8	7	6	5	4	3	2	1	0
reserved				ALIGN	EOCS	DDS	DMA	Reserved						CONT	ADON
				rw	rw	rw	rw							rw	rw

Fig.48

The ADC is powered on by setting bit 0 (ADON) bit in the ADC_CR2 register. When the ADON bit is set for the first time, it wakes up the ADC from the Power-down mode. In this code, ADON is set by the statement

machine.mem32[stm.ADC1 + stm.ADC_CR2] |= 0x1

Since the ADC1 should operate in Single conversion mode, bit 1 (CONT) must be cleared. After reset, CONT = 0, therefore we do nothing with it.

At the next step, we should select Channel 2 of ADC1 to process analog input signal. There are 16 multiplexed channels that could be organized in two groups: regular and injected. A group consists of a sequence of conversions that can be done on any channel and in any order.
For example, the conversion sequence may be in the following order:
ADC_IN3, ADC_IN8, ADC_IN2, ADC_IN2, ADC_IN0, ADC_IN2, ADC_IN2, ADC_IN15.
In this example, we will compose a regular group that includes a single conversion ADC_IN2 that corresponds to Channel 2. The regular channels and their order in the conversion sequence must be selected in the ADC_SQRx registers. The total number of conversions (=1, in our case) in the regular group must be written in the L[3:0] bits in the ADC_SQR1 register.
To set up the regular group in our code, we use two statements:

machine.mem32[stm.ADC1 + stm.ADC_SQR1] &= ~(0xf << 20)
machine.mem32[stm.ADC1 + stm.ADC_SQR3] |= 0x2

Then the code performs conversions with 5 s interval within the endless **while True** loop.
Each iteration begins with the statement

machine.mem32[stm.ADC1 + stm.ADC_CR2] |= 0x1 << 30

that starts the conversion by setting bit SWSTART in register ADC_CR2 (see **Fig.48**).
The end of conversion will be indicated by bit EOC (bit 2) in the ADC status register (ADC_SR) (**Fig.49**).

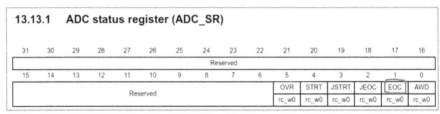

Fig.49

The following statement checks if bit EOC is set:

while (machine.mem32[stm.ADC1 + stm.ADC_SR] & 0x2) == 0:
    continue

If bit EOC = 1, we can move the result held in the ADC regular data register (ADC_DR) into variable **Dn** for further processing by the statement

Dn = machine.mem32[stm.ADC1 + stm.ADC_DR] & 0xfff

Then the voltage on the Channel 2 input is displayed on the screen.

Let's think of how to achieve better performance of our code (without taking into consideration the **print()** function). The code includes a few statements that can be rewritten in an inline assembler. The modified version of the previous code is shown in **Listing 74**.

Listing 74.

from pyb import Pin
import time

```python
a1_in2 = Pin('X3', Pin.ANALOG)
machine.mem32[stm.RCC + stm.RCC_APB2ENR] |= 1 << 8
machine.mem32[stm.ADC1 + stm.ADC_CR2] |= 0x1
machine.mem32[stm.ADC1 + stm.ADC_SQR1] &= ~(0xf << 20)
machine.mem32[stm.ADC1 + stm.ADC_SQR3] |= 0x2
Dn = 0
vin = 0.0
@micropython.asm_thumb
def start_conv():
    movwt(r0, stm.ADC1)
    ldr(r1, [r0, stm.ADC_CR2])
    movwt(r2, 0x1<<30)
    orr(r1, r2)
    str(r1, [r0, stm.ADC_CR2])
    movw(r2, 0x2)
    label(next_check)
    ldr(r1, [r0, stm.ADC_SR])
    and_(r1, r2)
    cmp(r1, 0)
    beq(next_check)
while True:
    start_conv()
    Dn = machine.mem32[stm.ADC1 + stm.ADC_DR] & 0xfff
    vin = Dn * 3.33 / 4095
    print("ADC1 CH2 Input = %2.3f V" % vin)
    time.sleep(5)
```

One more method to increase the performance of A/D conversion is to put ADC1 in Continuous conversion mode. In Continuous conversion mode, the ADC starts a new conversion as soon as it finishes one.

This mode is started with the CONT bit = 1 either by external trigger or by setting the SWSTART bit in the ADC_CR2 register (for regular channels only).

After each conversion for a regular group of channels is complete, the following actions occur:

- the last converted data are stored into the 16-bit ADC_DR register;
- the EOC (end of conversion) flag is set;
- an interrupt is generated if the EOCIE bit is set.

As compared with Single conversion mode, the SWSTART bit should be set only once, before the first conversion begins. Therefore, when we need to read analog input in a loop many times, Continuous conversion mode provides better performance.

The following example for PYBv1.1 (**Listing 75**) illustrates measuring an analog signal on ADC1 Channel 2 input using Continuous conversion mode.

Listing 75.

```
import time
machine.mem32[stm.GPIOA + stm.GPIO_MODER] |= 0b11 << 4
machine.mem32[stm.RCC + stm.RCC_APB2ENR] |= 1 << 8
machine.mem32[stm.ADC1 + stm.ADC_CR2] |= 0b11
machine.mem32[stm.ADC1 + stm.ADC_SQR1] &= ~(0xf << 20)
machine.mem32[stm.ADC1 + stm.ADC_SQR3] |= 0x2
Dn = 0
vin = 0.0
machine.mem32[stm.ADC1 + stm.ADC_CR2] |= 0x1 << 30
while True:
    while machine.mem32[stm.ADC1 + stm.ADC_SR] & 0x2 == 0:
        continue
    Dn = machine.mem32[stm.ADC1 + stm.ADC_DR] & 0xfff
    vin = Dn * 3.33 / 4095
    print("ADC1 CH2 Input = %2.3f V" % vin)
    time.sleep(5)
```

In this code, the statement

```
machine.mem32[stm.ADC1 + stm.ADC_CR2] |= 0b11
```

puts ADC1 in Continuous conversion mode. To start conversions, the statement

```
machine.mem32[stm.ADC1 + stm.ADC_CR2] |= 0x1 << 30
```

is executed before the **while True** loop is entered.

The similar code (**Listing 76**) will work on the STM32F4DISCOVERY board. Here we use ADC Channel 3 that is assigned pin PA3.

Listing 76.

```
import time
machine.mem32[stm.GPIOA + stm.GPIO_MODER] |= 0b11 << 6
machine.mem32[stm.RCC + stm.RCC_APB2ENR] |= 1 << 8
machine.mem32[stm.ADC1 + stm.ADC_CR2] |= 0b11
machine.mem32[stm.ADC1 + stm.ADC_SQR1] &= ~(0xf << 20)
machine.mem32[stm.ADC1 + stm.ADC_SQR3] |= 0x3
machine.mem32[stm.ADC1 + stm.ADC_SMPR2] |= 0b001 << 6
Dn = 0
vin = 0.0
machine.mem32[stm.ADC1 + stm.ADC_CR2] |= 0x1 << 30
while True:
    while machine.mem32[stm.ADC1 + stm.ADC_SR] & 0x2  == 0:
        continue
    Dn = machine.mem32[stm.ADC1 + stm.ADC_DR] & 0xfff
    vin = Dn * 3.00 / 4095
    print("ADC1 CH3 Input = %2.3f V" % vin)
    time.sleep(10)
```

One more approach to achieve better performance of A/D conversion is to reduce the ADC resolution (if acceptable) through the RES bits in the ADC control register 1 (ADC_CR1) (**Fig.50**).

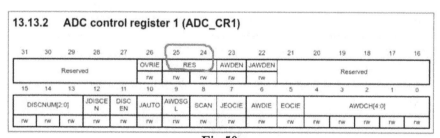

Fig.50

These bits are used to select the number of bits available in the data register. The minimum conversion time for each resolution is then as follows:
- 12 bits: 3 + 12 = 15 ADCCLK cycles;
- 10 bits: 3 + 10 = 13 ADCCLK cycles;
- 8 bits: 3 + 8 = 11 ADCCLK cycles;
- 6 bits: 3 + 6 = 9 ADCCLK cycles.

The following example (**Listing 77**) illustrates A/D conversion with 10-bit resolution.

Listing 77.

```
import time
machine.mem32[stm.GPIOA + stm.GPIO_MODER] |= 0b11 << 4
machine.mem32[stm.RCC + stm.RCC_APB2ENR] |= 1 << 8
machine.mem32[stm.ADC1 + stm.ADC_CR2] |= 0b11
machine.mem32[stm.ADC1 + stm.ADC_CR1] |= 0b01 << 24
machine.mem32[stm.ADC1 + stm.ADC_SQR1] &= ~(0xf << 20)
machine.mem32[stm.ADC1 + stm.ADC_SQR3] |= 0x2
Dn = 0
vin = 0.0
machine.mem32[stm.ADC1 + stm.ADC_CR2] |= 0x1 << 30
while True:
    while machine.mem32[stm.ADC1 + stm.ADC_SR] & 0x2 == 0:
        continue
    Dn = machine.mem32[stm.ADC1 + stm.ADC_DR] & 0x3ff
    vin = Dn * 3.33 / 1024
    print("ADC1 CH2 Input = %2.3f V" % vin)
    time.sleep(5)
```

In this code, the 10-bit resolution is set by the statement

machine.mem32[stm.ADC1 + stm.ADC_CR1] |= 0b01 << 24

Note that in this code we assume that the default resolution is 12-bit (bits RES[25:24] = 00).
With the 10-bit resolution, we should also modify the contents of the ADC data register ADC_DR as follows:

Dn = machine.mem32[stm.ADC1 + stm.ADC_DR] & 0x3ff

The final result of conversion kept in variable **vin** should be calculated as:

vin = Dn * 3.33 / 1024

To achieve the better precision of A/D conversion, we can increase the number cycles for sampling input data. The ADC samples the input voltage for a number of ADCCLK cycles that can be modified using the SMP[2:0] bits in the ADC_SMPR1 and ADC_SMPR2 registers. Each channel can be sampled with a different sampling time.

The total conversion time T is calculated as follows:

T = Sampling time + 12 cycles

Obviously, the performance of conversions will reduce as the number of cycles increases. The below code (**Listing 78**) allows to perform A/D conversion during 15 cycles. In this code, we use Single conversion mode.

Listing 78.

```
import time
machine.mem32[stm.GPIOA + stm.GPIO_MODER] |= 0b11 << 4
machine.mem32[stm.RCC + stm.RCC_APB2ENR] |= 1 << 8
machine.mem32[stm.ADC1 + stm.ADC_CR2] |= 0b1
machine.mem32[stm.ADC1 + stm.ADC_SQR1] &= ~(0xf << 20)
machine.mem32[stm.ADC1 + stm.ADC_SQR3] |= 0x2
machine.mem32[stm.ADC1 + stm.ADC_SMPR2] |= 0b001 << 6
Dn = 0
vin = 0.0
while True:
    machine.mem32[stm.ADC1 + stm.ADC_CR2] |= 0x1 << 30
    while machine.mem32[stm.ADC1 + stm.ADC_SR] & 0x2 == 0:
        continue
    Dn = machine.mem32[stm.ADC1 + stm.ADC_DR] & 0xfff
    vin = Dn * 3.33 / 4095
    print("ADC1 CH2 Input = %2.3f V" % vin)
    time.sleep(10)
```

In this code, the sampling time (=15 cycles) for ADC1 Channel 2 is configured by the following statement:

```
machine.mem32[stm.ADC1 + stm.ADC_SMPR2] |= 0b001 << 6
```

To increase the performance of applications while leaving high precision, we can rewrite the demo code from **Listing 78** so that it can operate in

Continuous conversion mode. Additionally, we will write the critical sections of code in an inline assembler. The modified version of the previous code is shown in **Listing 79**.

Listing 79.

```
import time
@micropython.asm_thumb
def get_adc_res():
    movwt(r0, stm.ADC1)
    movw(r2, 0x2)
    label(next_check)
    ldr(r1, [r0, stm.ADC_SR])
    and_(r1, r2)
    cmp(r1, 0)
    beq(next_check)
    ldr(r0, [r0, stm.ADC_DR])
    movw(r1, 0xfff)
    and_(r0, r1)
machine.mem32[stm.GPIOA + stm.GPIO_MODER] |= 0b11 << 4
machine.mem32[stm.RCC + stm.RCC_APB2ENR] |= 1 << 8
machine.mem32[stm.ADC1 + stm.ADC_CR2] |= 0b11
machine.mem32[stm.ADC1 + stm.ADC_SQR1] &= ~(0xf << 20)
machine.mem32[stm.ADC1 + stm.ADC_SQR3] |= 0x2
machine.mem32[stm.ADC1 + stm.ADC_SMPR2] |= 0b001 << 6
Dn = 0
vin = 0.0
machine.mem32[stm.ADC1 + stm.ADC_CR2] |= 0x1 << 30
while True:
    Dn = get_adc_res()
    vin = Dn * 3.33 / 4095
    print("ADC1 CH2 Input = %2.3f V" % vin)
    time.sleep(10)
```

Often it is convenient to trigger A/D Conversion by an external event (e.g. timer capture, overflow/underflow, EXTI line). For regular conversions, we can configure ADC1 device to be driven by external events through two group of bits, EXTEN[1:0] and EXTSEL[3:0] in the ADC control register 2 (ADC_CR2) (**Fig.51**).

13.13.3　ADC control register 2 (ADC_CR2)

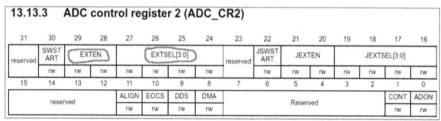

31	30	29	28	27	26	25	24	23	22	21	20	19	18	17	16
reserved	SWST ART	EXTEN			EXTSEL[3:0]			reserved	JSWST ART	JEXTEN			JEXTSEL[3:0]		
	rw	rw	rw	rw	rw	rw	rw		rw	rw	rw	rw	rw	rw	rw

15	14	13	12	11	10	9	8	7	6	5	4	3	2	1	0
reserved				ALIGN	EOCS	DDS	DMA		Reserved					CONT	ADON
				rw	rw	rw	rw							rw	rw

Fig.51

The role of EXTEN and EXTSEL bits becomes clear if we look at the fragment of a single ADC block (**Fig.52**).

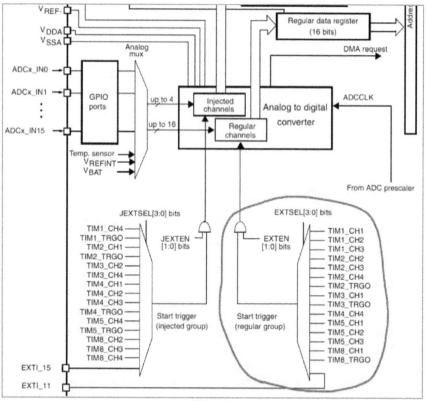

Fig.52

In this diagram, the EXTSEL bits switch the trigger inputs of multiplexer, while the EXTEN bits enable/disable the output of multiplexer.

If the EXTEN[1:0] control bits (for a regular conversion) or JEXTEN[1:0] bits (for an injected conversion) are different from 0b00, then external events are able to trigger A/D conversion with the selected polarity. The Table 67 from the STM32F405/407 MCU Reference Manual (**Fig.53**) provides the assignments for EXTEN[1:0] bits depending on the trigger polarity.

Table 67. Configuring the trigger polarity	
Source	**EXTEN[1:0] / JEXTEN[1:0]**
Trigger detection disabled	00
Detection on the rising edge	01
Detection on the falling edge	10
Detection on both the rising and falling edges	11

Fig.53

In the next example code, we select the rising edge for trigger polarity that corresponds to combination 0b01 of bits EXTEN[1:0]. Note that the polarity of the external trigger can be changed 'on the fly'.

The EXTSEL[3:0] control bits are used to select which out of 16 possible events can trigger conversion for the regular and injected groups. The Table 68 from STM32F405/407 Reference Manual (**Fig.54**) gives the possible external triggers for regular conversion.

Table 68. External trigger for regular channels		
Source	Type	EXTSEL[3:0]
TIM1_CH1 event		0000
TIM1_CH2 event		0001
TIM1_CH3 event		0010
TIM2_CH2 event		0011
TIM2_CH3 event		0100
TIM2_CH4 event		0101
TIM2_TRGO event	Internal signal from on-chip timers	0110
TIM3_CH1 event		0111
TIM3_TRGO event		1000
TIM4_CH4 event		1001
TIM5_CH1 event		1010
TIM5_CH2 event		1011
TIM5_CH3 event		1100
TIM8_CH1 event		1101
TIM8_TRGO event		1110
EXTI line11	External pin	1111

Fig.54

As a trigger source for our next example, we select TIM2_TRGO event that corresponds to combination 0b0110 of bits EXTSEL[3:0].
We must also allow Timer 2 to provide a trigger output (TRGO) to ADC when an update event (Timer 7 overflow) occurs. This can be done through configuring bits MMS[2:0] in the TIM2 control register 2 (TIM_CR2) (**Fig.55**).

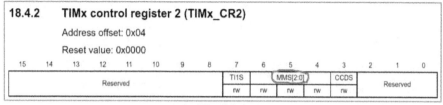

Fig.55

For our example, we select the combination 0b010 for bits MMS[2:0]. The application will run on PYBv1.1 and perform a single A/D conversion on

ADC1 Channel 2 every 10 s. This interval is determined by Timer 2 that is selected as a trigger to start the A/D conversion. The ADC1 will operate in Single conversion mode.
The MicroPython code for this application is shown in **Listing 80**.

Listing 80.

```
from pyb import Timer
tim2 = Timer(2, freq=0.1)
machine.mem32[stm.TIM2 + stm.TIM_CR2] &= ~(0b111 << 4)
machine.mem32[stm.TIM2 + stm.TIM_CR2] |= 0b010 << 4
machine.mem32[stm.GPIOA + stm.GPIO_MODER] |= 0b11 << 4
machine.mem32[stm.RCC + stm.RCC_APB2ENR] |= 1 << 8
machine.mem32[stm.ADC1 + stm.ADC_CR2] |= 0b1
machine.mem32[stm.ADC1 + stm.ADC_CR2] |= 0b01 << 28
machine.mem32[stm.ADC1 + stm.ADC_CR2] |= 0b0110 << 24
machine.mem32[stm.ADC1 + stm.ADC_SQR1] &= ~(0xf << 20)
machine.mem32[stm.ADC1 + stm.ADC_SQR3] |= 0x2
machine.mem32[stm.ADC1 + stm.ADC_SMPR2] |= 0b001 << 6
Dn = 0
vin = 0.0
while True:
    while machine.mem32[stm.ADC1 + stm.ADC_SR] & 0x2  == 0:
        continue
    Dn = machine.mem32[stm.ADC1 + stm.ADC_DR] & 0xfff
    vin = Dn * 3.33 / 4095
    print("ADC1 CH2 Input = %2.3f V" % vin)
```

In this code, we configure Timer 2 by the sequence

```
tim2 = Timer(2, freq=0.1)
machine.mem32[stm.TIM2 + stm.TIM_CR2] &= ~(0b111 << 4)
machine.mem32[stm.TIM2 + stm.TIM_CR2] |= 0b010 << 4
```

The frequency of Timer 2 overflow is selected to be 0.1 Hz that corresponds to the period of 10 s. Also we assign the value 0b010 to the MMS[2:0].
At the next step, we configure pin PA2 as input for ADC1 Channel 2 by the statement

```
machine.mem32[stm.GPIOA + stm.GPIO_MODER] |= 0b11 << 4
```

The rest of statements is already discussed in the previous examples. In this code, we don't need to use bit SWSTART that begins the A/D conversion – each conversion is started by Timer 2 TRGO output every 10 s.

The similar code (**Listing 81**) will measure the input voltage on ADC1 Channel 3 (pin PA3) of the STM32F4DISCOVERY board.

Listing 81.

```
from pyb import Timer
tim2 = Timer(2, freq=0.1)
machine.mem32[stm.TIM2 + stm.TIM_CR2] &= ~(0b111 << 4)
machine.mem32[stm.TIM2 + stm.TIM_CR2] |= 0b010 << 4
machine.mem32[stm.GPIOA + stm.GPIO_MODER] |= 0b11 << 6
machine.mem32[stm.RCC + stm.RCC_APB2ENR] |= 1 << 8
machine.mem32[stm.ADC1 + stm.ADC_CR2] |= 0b1
machine.mem32[stm.ADC1 + stm.ADC_CR2] |= 0b01 << 28
machine.mem32[stm.ADC1 + stm.ADC_CR2] |= 0b0110 << 24
machine.mem32[stm.ADC1 + stm.ADC_SQR1] &= ~(0xf << 20)
machine.mem32[stm.ADC1 + stm.ADC_SQR3] |= 0x3
machine.mem32[stm.ADC1 + stm.ADC_SMPR2] |= 0b001 << 6
Dn = 0
vin = 0.0
while True:
    while machine.mem32[stm.ADC1 + stm.ADC_SR] & 0x2  == 0:
        continue
    Dn = machine.mem32[stm.ADC1 + stm.ADC_DR] & 0xfff
    vin = Dn * 3.0 / 4095
    print("ADC1 CH3 Input = %2.3f V" % vin)
```

We can also trigger ADC using external interrupt on line 11. In this case, the rising / falling edge on the dedicated pin (PA11, PB11, PC11, etc.) can start A/D conversion.
The following code (**Listing 82**) written for PYBv1.1 starts conversion on ADC1 Channel 2 by bringing pin PB11 ('Y10') HIGH (rising edge) every 10 s. The ADC1 operates in Single conversion mode.

Listing 82.

```
from pyb import Pin, ExtInt
def ext11_isr(param):
    return
ext11 = ExtInt(Pin('Y10'), ExtInt.IRQ_RISING, \
Pin.PULL_NONE, ext11_isr)

machine.mem32[stm.TIM2 + stm.TIM_CR2] &= ~(0b111 << 4)
machine.mem32[stm.TIM2 + stm.TIM_CR2] |= 0b010 << 4
machine.mem32[stm.GPIOA + stm.GPIO_MODER] |= 0b11 << 4
machine.mem32[stm.RCC + stm.RCC_APB2ENR] |= 1 << 8
machine.mem32[stm.ADC1 + stm.ADC_CR2] |= 0b1
machine.mem32[stm.ADC1 + stm.ADC_CR2] |= 0b01 << 28
machine.mem32[stm.ADC1 + stm.ADC_CR2] |= 0b1111 << 24
machine.mem32[stm.ADC1 + stm.ADC_SQR1] &= ~(0xf << 20)
machine.mem32[stm.ADC1 + stm.ADC_SQR3] |= 0x2
machine.mem32[stm.ADC1 + stm.ADC_SMPR2] |= 0b001 << 6

Dn = 0
vin = 0.0
while True:
    while machine.mem32[stm.ADC1 + stm.ADC_SR] & 0x2 == 0:
        continue
    Dn = machine.mem32[stm.ADC1 + stm.ADC_DR] & 0xfff
    vin = Dn * 3.33 / 4095
    print("ADC1 CH2 Input = %2.3f V" % vin)
```

In order to control ADC through the interrupt line 11 (EXTI_11), we should first configure the external interrupt on the selected pin (PB11 or 'Y10') using the sequence:

```
def ext11_isr(param):
    return
ext11 = ExtInt(Pin('Y10'), ExtInt.IRQ_RISING, \
Pin.PULL_NONE, ext11_isr)
```

The rest of code relates to configuring ADC1 Channel 2. The configuration sequence is almost the same as that in the previous example, except configuring bits EXTSEL[3:0] in register ADC_CR2. These bits should be assigned the value 0b1111 (see **Fig.54**). That is done by the statement machine.mem32[stm.ADC1 + stm.ADC_CR2] |= 0b1111 << 24

Again, we don't need to start ADC by setting SWSTART bit.

Conclusion

As it has been mentioned in this book, all example codes can easily be adapted for any board equipped with STM32F4xx MCU. The author successfully tested the MicroPython example codes on the NUCLEO-L476 and NETDUINO PLUS 2 boards so the readers can adapt and use these tools while testing all code examples from this book.

Index

A

A/D resolution, 126
alternate function, 86, 96, 103
analog-to-digital conversion (ADC), 118

C

class Pin, 19
Continuous A/D conversion mode, 124

D

DfuSe utility, 10, 12
digital-to-analog converter (DAC), 105
Direct Memory Access (DMA), 106

E

effective address, 40

I

inline assembler, 17
Input Capture mode, 83, 94
Interrupt Service Routine (ISR), 53, 54
it instruction, 58

M

machine module, 17
memory-mapped registers, 18

N

non-blocking delay, 69

P

physical address, 39
pop instruction, 56
prescaler, 71
push instruction, 56
PWM, 95
PYBv1.1, 10

R

real-time clock (RTC), 72, 92

S

Single A/D conversion mode, 119
stm module, 20

T

timer, 68

www.ingramcontent.com/pod-product-compliance
Lightning Source LLC
Chambersburg PA
CBHW052147070326
40689CB00050B/2343